Founder

Prevention & Cure
the natural way

Related works by Jaime Jackson:

Books:
The Natural Horse: Lessons from the Wild (1992) - 1st edition
The Natural Horse: Foundations For Natural Horsemanship (1997) - 2nd edition
Horse Owners Guide to Natural Hoof Care (1999) - 1st edition
Horse Owners Guide to Natural Hoof Care (2002) - Revised edition
Founder – Prevention & Cure the Natural Way (2001)
Guide To Booting Horses For Natural Hoof Care Practitioners (2001)

Videos:
Learn to Do A Natural Trim With Jaime Jackson:
    Creating the Perfect Hoof (2000)
Guide To Booting Horses For Natural Hoof Care Practitioners (2001)

Articles — American Farriers Journal
"Spirit of the Natural Horse," Jan/Feb, 1992.
"Forging the Naturally Shaped Hoof," Dec, 1992.
"The Naturally Shaped Hoof," Sep/Oct, 1992.
"The Natural Draft Horse Hoof," Sep/Oct, 1993.
"Mule Hooves In The Outback," Jul/Aug, 1993.
"Naturally Colored Hooves–White Hooves In the Wild," May/Jun, 1993.
"Going Barefooted," Dec, 1997.
"Hoof Balance . . . Getting In Step With Nature's Way," Jan/Feb, 1994.

Founder

Prevention & Cure
the natural way

by Jaime Jackson

found·er² (foun´dar), *v.i.* **1.** to stum-
ble, break down, or go lame, as a
horse. —*v.t.* **2.** *Vet. Pathol.* to cause (a
horse) to break down, go lame, or suffer
from laminitis [MF: *(fondr(er)* (to) plunge
to the bottom < L *fund(us)* bottom]

STAR RIDGE PUBLISHING

Star Ridge Publishing
P.O. Box 2181
Harrison, AR 72601

1-870-743-4603
1-870-743-1637 (FAX)
e-mail: star@star-ridge.com
on-line: www.star-ridge.com

To contact Jaime Jackson:
star100@alltel.net

Cover illustration from the German text, "Der Huf" by H. Ruthe, 1959.

Table of Contents

Primum non nocere — vis medicatrix naturae.
First, do no harm — honor the healing powers of nature. — Hippocrates

Preface to 2003 Edition

This 2003 edition of *Founder* marks the 3rd printing by Star Ridge Publishing. Many readers have asked why I never included "trimming guidelines" in this book, given the complexities of a laminitis-deformed hoof capsule. The reason is simple, although ostensibly not obvious: *we will simply do a natural trim.* After all, if we aren't going to trim the hoof "naturally", then what are we going to do, and what good then is natural hoof care?

My first book on natural hoof care, *Horse Owners Guide To Natural Hoof Care*, is certainly not irrelevant on the subject of trimming laminitic horses. It provides the general guidelines for the natural trim and related natural horse-keeping practices, and practitioners should therefore give it diligent study. Unfortunately, the deformed laminitic capsule can terrorize and obfuscate the uninitiated eye to the natural hoof within. Obscured too are the native healing mechanisms which restore the capsule and the animal's soundness. Consequently, what is actually a straight-forward process, natural trimming accompanied by natural healing, becomes to the untrained and inexperienced, an unintelligible if not impossible roadmap for therapeutic hoof care.

In my natural hoof care clinics, wherein virtually all the hooves (cadavers) I train with, are laminitic, experience has taught me that most students, to surmount the complexities of the deformed capsule, need a clearer picture of the steps involved in natural trimming then what I've provided in the general guidelines (HOG). An important part of this picture includes our recognition and understanding of the hoof's "healing angle-of-growth", or H°. Much of the hoof care providing community is now either unaware of, or at war with, this most significant dynamic of natural healing. Teaching H° now lies at the core of all my instruction as a clinician.

While the clinic environment is a very effective and highly recommended way to convey a better understanding of what is involved, including trimming to H°, it is not always feasible for practitioners to travel to my home state (AR) to learn. Thus, to help close the gap—to render the natural hoof care map more accessible and useful—I've developed a new article series: the Star Ridge Natural Hoof Care Bulletins. These articles, augmented by new companion videos, provide highly specialized trimming guidelines premised on H°. Three bulletins alone are dedicated specifically to the elucidation of laminitis pathophysiology; the inherent natural healing mechanisms we must work with and not against; and the technical procedures I recommend for reversing the immediate effects of acute laminitis, while rolling back the long term damage plaguing the deformed (chronic) laminitic hoof. To learn more about these, I encourage the reader or practitioner struggling with laminitic horses to reference the Resource section of this book for specifics.

— Jaime Jackson

Prologue in the Warner Mountains

April, 1984, midnight, Hayward, California

"Jaime, it's Willard. I think you'll want to come and see this. Get up here as quick as you can. We've never seen this sort of thing happen before. It's over on Sand Flat, off the Modoc HMA,[†] 50 miles south of Devil's Garden. A band — a stud, his son, and three mares — they've got into a fenced riparian area. We don't know how long they've been in there. It's just terrible . . . we're gonna have to take them out right away. You'd better come up tonight."

Bill ("Willard") S. had always been a good BLM (Bureau of Land Management) contact for me. He'd helped me find my way to the first bands several years earlier. Always alerted me to the gathers. Government guys like Willard knew the herds well, how to find them, how to get close to them. And when I wanted to do the hoof measurements, the research, he'd been there for me too. He had made it all right with the wranglers, the vets, and the other Wild Horse Management Specialists like himself. So they'd help me hold the horses a little longer on the ground, or in the chutes, or on those tilt tables, so I could do my work, measuring the hooves.

And now, here he was calling me in the middle of the night about a band of mustangs out in the middle of nowhere. I didn't ask him what it was about, specifically. If it was important enough in Willard's mind to call me at this hour, then it was important enough for me to get up there and find out.

So, I just packed up a few belongings and headed north from

[†]Herd Management Area

the Bay Area. I was there before the sun came up.

Sand Flat lies low in the long chain of mountains known as the Warner Range, which runs along the northeastern edge of California, adjacent to Nevada. This is the western edge of wild horse country. Sand Flat is situated on the southwestern flank of the Warners, below a federal wilderness area. It lies at the bottom of an alluvial gorge, cut deep here and there by icy, winter streams gushing out of the forested reaches far above. Wild horses seldom frequent this area, or at least seldom stay, preferring their haunts further east in the Great Basin.

Eagle Peak, highest and most stately prince of the Warners, is up in there somewhere too, a great magnet for snow, rising 13,000 feet above the rocky, high desert floor. Shedding its white cap each spring, myriad rivulets cascade ever downward upon its western slopes. Some of the more pronounced gushes eventually zigzag and pierce their way into Sand Flat, gouging out here and there cut

banks in the desolate, virtually uninhabited lunar-like landscape. Several of these, due to the igneous bedrock supporting them, have, aided by an abundance of fertile alluvial soil, given birth to several important vegetative systems. These are the riparians, or so they are called by government biologists who have brought them under protective custody.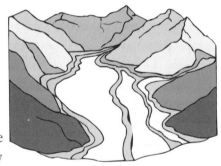

The riparians are home to lush grasses and water-laden plants, who owe their oasis-like existence in an otherwise barren homeland — not unlike the fertile strip bordering the Nile River) — to the availability of mountain water, which only several yards to either side, is sucked dry as though it never existed.

It wasn't always this way on Sand Flat. Not half a decade before, a hundred year old cattle ranching and strip mining legacy had denuded the landscape, wasting the riparians — or rather, precluded their 20th Century existence — which had once quenched the thirsts of Paiute Indian hunters before the coming of the white man. Now, the Department of the Interior, headmaster of the BLM, bowing to fierce political pressure from unrelenting environmentalists, had closed off (by means of barbed wire fencing) a few of these unique ecological niches dotting the Sand Flat alluvial fan. And to one of them Willard and I were now en route via government jeep.

We arrived as the first glow of sunlight radiated from behind the wall of mountains directly in our path. I remember that the old jeep leaked in the cold morning air, and its heater either didn't work or wasn't worth a hang. It didn't seem to phase Willard, but I just sat there shivering as we bumped along, relieved when we at last arrived at our destination so I could get out and move.

It's still not clear to me nearly 20 years later how it happened. But the band had somehow penetrated the fence line and entered the half mile riparian strip. Maybe they were driven in there by locals, dissident ranchers angered by the ecology types who've seen to it that their cattle can no longer ravage the land within the fence line. Now the horses would do their dirty work. Whatever, once hemmed in, and significantly out of sight of human eyes, till now, as it were, they had also entered a kind of ersatz horse's paradise. Lush, sweet, knee-high grass, endless browse, cool clean water, mineral deposits for salt-lick, warm sand for rolling, the absence of competitors — equid or otherwise. To the point, I mean, they had absolutely no incentive to leave.

"Look at them," broke in Willard, "every one of them is lame."

This is what Willard wanted me to see. It was clear, abundantly obvious in fact, that every one of them had foundered.

"What do you make of it, Jaime." He enquired. "I know this band from last year when they were on the eastern range. None of them were lame. In twenty years that I've known them, this has never happened."

I speculated: "Maybe it's the lush grass. Or the plants. Or something in the water." I didn't know. All I knew is that they were dead lame. And laminitic. Wild horses, for all I knew up until then, seldom suffered debilitating lamenesses, certainly nothing like this. Maybe a fall, a broken leg, or a twisted ankle, but never founder. No one who knows the wild ones had heard of it, spoken of it, or believed it could happen in mustang country. But it did.

Scanning the outlying area, I now spotted three skittish bachelors about 300 yards off in the dry land. The wild ones had taught me how to approach them, even these satellite stallion groups. So I grabbed my binoculars and made my way closer to them. They were unfoundered.

I thanked Willard for the experience and he drove me back to his field station.

I thought about the lush, green grass as I drove back to the Bay Area. Could it really have been the cause? I mean, how could green grass harm horses' feet? Especially wild ones? All across wild horse country, mustangs frequent grassy edged streams for water, with no apparent lameness. If the grass was so bad for them, then they would be foundering too, like the Sand Flat band. But I've been all over out there in wild horse country. And that isn't the case. They don't founder.

A month later, back at my own work as a farrier, I couldn't let the experience go. I know of many horses who live on the green. "Nothing happens to them, does it?" I thought aloud to myself, for a moment blanking out all those fat, "cresty" necked exceptions with stretched white lines all farriers are aware of. The Sand Flat episode had to have been a fluke with an explanation. Maybe there was something in the water in that cut bank. Maybe it was some kind of plant growing on the moist bank of the riparian. My mind just clouded over.

Willard and several wranglers opened the fence and released the entire band, after I left that day. I never did find out what happened to them, although I've wondered about it all these years. Willard died only a few years later. I think just a few months before he was to retire. He didn't have any kids. In fact, he never married in his entire life. He just loved his work, loved being in the high desert mountains, and loved knowing the wild ones.

Foreword: lost in the founder shuffle

Founder is a response to toxicity. For a natural healing to ensue, the horse's body and his feet must be purged holistically of toxins. Diet, movement, environment, socialization, everything touching the horse's life. These things must be scrutinized, and the toxic offender isolated and removed. No stone can be left unturned. It's something we — the horse owners — must do for our horses. No one can do it for us. And this will require clear thinking and a different set of truths then we've held previously. — Jaime Jackson

All truth passes through three stages. First, it is ridiculed. Second, it is violently opposed. Third, it is accepted as being self-evident. — Arthur Scopenhauer (1788-1860)

This little book has been created to help horse owners save their horses from a deadly killer and lamer, *founder*. It was written especially for horse owners seeking a natural, effective, and inexpensive alternative to expensive conventional founder treatments. The latter can be as debilitating and deadly as the pathology itself.

I've been a professional farrier since the 1970s, and a "barefoot" advocate and practitioner in more recent years. By barefoot, I mean that the horse's feet are provided with what I call a "natural trim" and are then conditioned — toughened up, in other words — to go without horseshoes. Contrary to popular belief, barefootedness isn't harmful to horses. Nature intended for horses to go barefooted! I mention this because it has been precisely my experience with barefooted horses that has led me directly to a natural cure for founder.

My earliest experience with barefooted horses didn't take place either with my clients' horses or with my own. In fact, it didn't even take place among domestic horses. Readers familiar with my first book, *The Natural Horse* (1992), will recall that I came to understand barefootedness through America's wild horses of the West: the mustang. In the full vigor of the horse's natural world,

Wild stallions clash with founder free hooves (SRP files)

the wild horse truly unveils the vision and reality of sound, high performance barefootedness to its fullest potential. Of course, the wild ones have never been shod. But they endure prolifically because their hooves *enable* their hardy lifestyles, there in the toughest of all known equine environments. The horse's hooves are meant to work, *and work hard*. To a person with half an open mind, it is impossible not to observe the wild ones grinding their hooves into the ground 24 hours a day and not ponder why it is that we feel so compelled to coddle our horses' feet in iron, when it is entirely unnecessary.

Founder is really unknown in wild horse country. The riparian incident aforementioned was man-made; nevertheless it provides a powerful clue in the unraveling of the founder mystery. Although I honestly didn't understand *why* it happened when confronted by the Sand Flat specter, the logic of natural prevention relative to natural lifestyles eventually came upon me. More than once, persons have suggested to me that wild horses are exempt from laminitis due to their inherited characteristics. Nothing could be further from the truth. *It is the lifestyle alone.*

To affect a founder cure, one must bring about the natural lifestyle conditions that preclude its outbreak in the first place. In the horse's natural world, prevention and cure are rolled into one. And on this note, I'd like you — particularly if your horse is suffering from laminitis — to contemplate an important premise of this book:

> *It is improbable, except largely through chance, to cure or prevent founder without knowing how we violate the horse's natural state, and doing something about it.*

No study exists which I'm aware of that reliably documents the number of conventionally treated foundered horses that are "cured", or that survive in limbo between soundness and lameness, or that go to slaughter. My many contacts with horse owners and professionals over the years suggest that the situation is not good. The statistics of founder, like many other hoof-based breakdowns, are swallowed in the larger black hole of lameness, where account-ability seems as unfathomable as remedies appear scant and un-forthcoming. Yet Walt Taylor, co-founder of the American Farri-ers Association, and a member of the World Farriers Association and Working Together for Equines programs, would testify only last year:

> Of the 122 million equines found around the world, no more than 10 percent are clinically sound. Some 10 percent (12.2 million) are clinically, completely and unusably lame. The re-maining 80 percent (97.6 million) of these equines are some-what lame . . . and could not pass a soundness evaluation or test. [American Farriers Journal, Nov./2000, v. 26, #6, p. 5.][†]

But I do know that horses can be cured of their founder, or the affliction outright prevented, if the horse owner only applies the necessary natural management changes to create an environment that is incongruous with founder pathogenesis. Surprisingly, this isn't hard to do. At least once one is properly informed of what's involved. This little book explains exactly what you need to do, what to avoid, and *why*. It also addresses *why* conventional veteri-nary/farriery procedures are so unsuccessful — in fact, counterpro-ductive to natural healing and prevention — yet remain the stan-dard *modus operandi* across the domestic horse using community.

What does happen to foundered horses in our midst?

Most horse owners, not harboring a distrust or suspicion of their professional agents providing conventional veterinary and far-riery care, and knowing nothing of the natural alternative de-

---

[†]To confuse the issue, earlier, in the May/June (2000) issue of the AFJ, pub-lisher Frank Lessiter reported from a 1998 U.S. Department of Agriculture study, "A survey of the U.S. horse population [6.9 million] indicates that over half of all equine operations had at least one horse with lameness problems dur-ing the previous year. Some 13 percent of horse operations had laminitis cases." It's hard to conjecture specific numbers from this finding, not knowing what constitutes an "equine operation" with "at least one" lameness issue. But if I were to venture a guess, I would say that at least a third of a million U.S. horses are currently foundered.

scribed in this book, launch directly into the usual venues of modern founder therapy when the laminitic attack is on. It is an expensive path to get on, and few horse owners can afford to take it all the way — to wherever that may be.

Many foundered horses, the worst cases, are put down immediately, their suffering so terrible, their owners unable to cope emotionally with the devastation. Others are doped up with powerful painkillers to mitigate the debilitating pain of the founder attack and its horrific aftermath, living for months on end on these chemicals until their digestive systems begin to ulcerate. Some horses seem to heal, then re-founder, and then re-founder again, and still again. Some are buted and shod to conceal the "stretched white line," and are then taken to the sale barn and sold to the unwitting, providing the killer buyer can be outbid.

Many foundered horses are turned out to pasture, if one is available, to let "nature take its course." Hopefully, a curative one. But even here the root cause may be ignored — including the rich green pasture itself! — and the founder cycles on unchecked regardless. Some horse owners, savvy in some measure to these idyllic founder "traps" come spring or fall, play cat and mouse with fescue foot by "dry-lotting" the poor horse when the grass starts to come on strong, hoping that they've caught the situation in time. Countless other foundered horses, however, fail in this game of Russian roulette, and consequently perish during "pasture turnouts" every year. And here I have a sad story by way of confirmation:

The owner of a large animal "carcass removal" company I procure cadaver hooves from for my hoof care seminars, told me in November of 1999, "The back-hoe operators have really put a dent in our business. Our local operator tells me he has made so much money in recent years burying dead horses on private property that he no longer contracts out for other kinds of work." Many of those horses were founder cases.

It is common for many foundered horses to become "breeders" if the animal is still "serviceable" and his genes are sufficiently coveted. This often includes mares, and occasionally stallions. The great racing Thoroughbred, Secretariat, comes immediately to mind, although he eventually succumbed (i.e., euthanasia) to founder — unnecessarily so, as it were, for if he had received the holistic care that is described in this book, I have no doubt he could have returned fully to the gallop within months of the date of his lethal injection.

At the far end of the spectrum of conventional "humane" care for lame or abused horses — before one enters the fringe of "alternative" therapies — are the burgeoning "rescue" organizations advertising nearly everywhere these days. Countless foundered horses are taken up by these groups, who, although well intentioned, may offer the horse nothing in the way of genuine natural lifestyle changes. So founder may traverse their camps with the same ravenous appetite for destruction as the more conventional veterinary ones.

Now I should mention that some horse owners, rigorously dedicated to saving their treasured horses, cannot accept either slaughter, the purgatories of perpetual lameness, or quite simply, the haunting specter of uncertainty. *They must know why founder happens and if there exists a genuine cure.* So they dig in and pursue far beyond the boundaries of the accepted but ineffectual conventions of veterinary medicine. There they hope to find something, *anything*, that can help save their horses. If you're one of them, then that's probably why you've stumbled upon this little book.

The pathogenesis (i.e., the pathological origin and development) of founder, like many equine lamenesses, is not well-understood in the domestic horse world. Typically, it is explained by horse owners and professionals alike in terms that skirt or disdain the significance or value of the horse's natural state — what we see in wild horse country. These "lessons from the wild," of course, are deemed irrelevant or are simply unknown to them because they have not read into the subject or have never been among wild horses to know what they are.

Consequently, founder is accounted in rather direct and immediate ways; for example: the horse was "too fat," had thyroid deficiency, or "he got into his grain and ate too much," or "was ridden too hard," or in such scientific terms as, "pathogens multiplying in his cecum produced a substance that activated lamellar enzymes which caused lamellar separation between the capsule and PIII," and so forth.

These kinds of explanations, while to the point very specific, in fact, only serve to prevent or postpone our inquiries into the deeper, more profound *causal* relationships between founder and the aforementioned lifestyle violations of the horse's native state. Let me explain.

It's not so much that the horse was "too fat" or "grain greedy," but that he was probably a victim of an unnatural diet that compelled him to overeat. Not unlike a person bingeing compulsively after abandoning a starvation diet. Both are starving. Moreover, it was likely that the kind and amount of grain he was being fed was not good for him either.

Nor is it likely that a thyroid imbalance was the cause, as much as an unbalanced (i.e., unnatural) lifestyle which lead to metabolic irregularities that, in turn, adversely impacted the thyroid gland.

Nor was the real issue that the horse was ridden too hard, but that he was probably shod and endowed with unnaturally shaped hooves that favored a laminitic reaction.

And finally, even the scientific explanation – pathogenic proliferation of harmful enzymes overwhelming the horse's feet, while correct (in large measure), in my opinion – really only confuses matters, and fails to help the horse owner. It does not give the reason for the multiplication of harmful pathogens in the horse's gut in the first place. Indeed, such explications become justification for prescribing potent chemical "inhibitors" that are either ineffectual or have other side effects egregious to the horse's already stressed out system.

Lost in the founder shuffle is the *holistic* perspective. Indeed, at the core of the founder problem is that horses are brought into entire regimens of unnatural care that violate their natural order.

Thus, while many aspects of their care are in fact co-conspirators in the pathogenesis of founder, the approach to treatment is usually approached unilaterally. "A" cause is searched out and treated specifically. As commonly, horses are given "specific" treatments (e.g., heart bar shoes) with little or no attention paid to causality. Larger, lifestyle issues, are commonly ignored or deemed irrelevant.

We can, and should, look at founder in terms of a lifestyle "scale." On one side there are natural lifestyle violations in various stages of prevalence and severity; on the other side, is the horse's health. As unnatural care builds on one side, the scale begins to tip precariously in favor of laminitic breakdown. Then, a single event – such as any of the above given in testimony – can tip the balance far enough to precipitate a laminitic attack. Many laminitic horses are brought to the brink of destruction, including death from shock or euthanasia, because treatment follows unilaterally along single events, rather than confronting the entire picture – and acting to change it. Acting within the larger picture, this book will show, will bring about the holistic cure of founder.

So, with holistic causality on the back burner, and natural care intervention still too remote to consider, conventional founder therapies are quickly put in place if the horse owner can afford them. Such treatments, in contrast to natural healing, are actually tantamount to building a sophisticated cantilever bridge across a one foot divide, when all one really needs to do is simply step across at a natural pace to get to the other side. The logic for building the bridge is faulty, and all the engineering and technology is completely unnecessary. Likewise, the therapeutic "bridges" veterinary and farriery practitioners normally build are unnecessary. They are a waste of time and money, and in my opinion, hazardous to the horse's health. Insidiously, they contraindicate the simple and effective alternative of natural, holistic based healing.

Of course, it's hard to think lucidly in such logical, "do this, don't do that," terms when one's horse is under the founder gun, agonizing in pain – and maybe getting ready to die from shock. You are understandably emotionally distressed and desperate. We are humans after all. Expectedly, we turn to our professionals who bring on the pain medications, blood thinners, padded shoes, and so forth! Urgency and the gravity of the situation demand immediate action.

Natural healing and prevention, although still virtually unheard of to date (Spring, 2001), should have their berth in the mainstream of founder therapies. Don't let anyone tell you otherwise. We just need to understand how natural healing works and then get on with it as quick as we can. Whether or not your horse is in the middle of an acute attack, or is hovering in partial recovery or remission, or even if he is still sound and has never been laminitic, it's never too late to get started . . . to get on the natural healing pathway.

How does one get started?

By becoming aware.

First, we must look beyond the distressing founder symptoms and into the realm of *causality*. Why does founder happen? And, just as important, when doesn't it happen? We'll need to learn about the horse's natural lifestyle to answer these questions. And our wild horses will help us.

Getting on the natural healing pathway is really as much a mental process, as it is a physical method of taking care of our horses more naturally. In fact, a friend of mine who advises human cancer victims regularly to make healthier lifestyle changes, believes this sort of thing always begins in our heads. We've got to see the "whole" picture first, before we can see what needs to be done with the parts that have gone wrong.

Why don't we take my friend's good advice and start there. Let's "clear our minds" of all this founder pathology just for a minute, and try to get a sense of the larger picture. Where we stand in it, and where we are going.

1 Clearing our minds

There are no outs, no scapegoats, no fall guys, no more saviors for us. Now, it is down to just us, you and I. We did it and we have to clean it up, stop it, change it, or let it go on as it is. No one, and I mean no one, is going to come down from anywhere and save our asses.
— Little Crow (*Sacred Hill Within – A Lakota World View*)

*I*n the small north Arkansas town where I live there is a quaint "health food" store where I shop occasionally. The owner, Todd, is a conscientious fellow always concerned as much about his fellow humans' health and eating habits as his own. Like the natural horse care movement, health food stores are magnets that draw determined people looking for "natural remedies" to personal health and dietary crises — some life threatening — that cannot be solved by conventional, mainstream medical therapies.

"Too often they arrive at our door after it's too late to help them, especially cancer victims," states Todd, who many also seek out for his reputation as a physical fitness buff. (Todd, muscular and fit, and a strict vegetarian, is also a body builder and several years ago won the Mr. Arkansas Body Building Gold Medal — I guess you could say he's our local Arnold Schwarzenegger!). I asked Todd what he tells people coming in looking for alternative solutions to serious, life-threatening diseases, like cancer. His response is always the same:

"I tell them to begin inside their heads. That by 'clearing our minds,' questioning why we do things, including doing things that we know aren't healthy, and asking ourselves if we can't change our ways, we will be able to identify and remove the causes of cancer."

Of course, most people avoid introspection of this sort, at least until they're sufficiently traumatized by something very serious, like cancer, or in our case, founder. Further, prevention normally isn't even an issue when nothing's wrong — why fix something if it isn't broken? But unless one places little or no value on life, most people get introspective very quickly when the problem, like cancer (or founder), strikes deeply at home. And hopefully before it's too late.

I get calls every week from horse owners around the country with horses that are stricken by founder. So I know exactly what Todd, and his clients, go through. It's terrible and, like Todd, I agonize with the people who come to me. If I didn't care, I wouldn't do this sort of work.

But Todd is right, the natural path begins by looking inside ourselves, into our beliefs, and into the nature of our habits, especially how those habits impact the way we care for our horses. Since they're completely at our mercy for their every need, that's a lot of personal responsibility at our command. Of course, we want the very best for our horses, but how we identify with them has a lot to do with the quality of care we ultimately provide them with. We can love our horses, think the world of them, and even provide them with everything we think they need. But still hurt them because we don't really understand their genuine needs and limits at all. We just think we do. And, unfortunately, for the foundered horse, that just isn't good enough.

Thinking again about cancer victims and how, in many cases, unhealthy or self-destructive behavior — such as smoking cigarettes — can lead to this disease, we are all reminded of people who smoke and have paid for it with their lives. Some of us may have forgotten, or are too young to know, but until the latter half of the 20th century, people commonly believed that smoking wasn't harmful to their health. They smoked, habitually, and loved it (not that many still don't!). People commonly offered cigarettes to others to "enjoy" their smokes with, spreading the toxic fumes wherever they went, even if others were annoyed by it and professed to know better.

Adults could "light up" anywhere, any time, as they pleased. In restaurants, in elevators, at work, even in doctors' offices where they might be checking up on a persistent cough! Indeed, smoking was raised to a near national virtue, advertised in every media, including the movies where such notable film stars as John Wayne, Susan Hayward, Humphrey Bogart, and Clark Gable — all dead from cancer precipitated by years of smoking — set an example for this perfectly acceptable social behavior. A deadly killer as it turns out.

Well, there's a parallel in "founder" pathogenesis. To those of us in the natural horse care movement, the act of unwittingly precipitating founder in horses is as obvious as sticking a cigarette in a person's mouth and believing it's a good thing to do. Indeed, we can introduce our children to smoking and kill them with cancer (state and federal laws now try to prevent this), and we can just as easily subject our horses to unhealthy practices we think are perfectly okay, but which in reality, cause them to founder. It's really that simple.

Founder, I've stated, stems from our ignorance of the horse's natural state. By "natural state," I mean the horse's natural lifeway as characterized by our free-roaming, wild horse populations. When we provide for the horse in ways that violate his native way, we upset his natural metabolism, which, in turn, provides a fertile bed for founder to sprout from. Founder, in this interpretation, is a lifestyle affliction.

Technically speaking, on one level, founder "sprouts" from an inflammation and breakdown of tiny leaf-like structures, called *lamina*. The lamina comb the outer surface of the coffin bone (*Distal phalanx*) within the hoof (or hoof capsule), and bind it to the inside or middle portion of the hoof wall (*Stratum medium*). The lamina, therefore, perform a suspensory function within the hoof, namely supporting the weight of the horse as it compresses downward upon the coffin bone and transfers across to the hoof wall proper.

Dr. Chris Pollit, a researcher at the Equine Medicine School of

Veterinary Medicine, University of Queensland, Australia, has studied extensively the pathological changes which the lamina undergo during laminitis. According to Pollit, closely related to the necrosis of the lamina, is the deterioration of an inner extracellular structure called the *basal membrane*. This membrane forms a bridge between the basal cells producing the lamina, on one side, and the connective tissue emanating from the surface of the coffin bone, on the other. Pollit writes:

> Laminin, one of the key proteins of the basement membrane, forms receptor sites and ligands for a complex array of growth factors, cytokines, adhesion molecules and integrins. Without an intact, functional, basement membrane, the epidermis [lamina], to which it is attached, falls into disarray. Significantly, disintegration and separation of the lamellar basement membrane is a feature of acute laminitis.[†]

Pollit believes that the proliferation of a certain class of enzymes, called *matrix metalloproteinases* (MMPs, for short), trigger the disorganization of the lamina, their basal cells, and the dissolution of the membrane, early in the laminitic attack. I would agree, and there is no doubt in my mind that MMPs arise from toxins produced by unnatural lifestyle conditions which have nothing to do with the horse's feet. Most of this book will address these conditions, as well as how to return the laminitic hoof to its natural, healthy form.

The "key" to curing and preventing founder, hence, lies in understanding its *causality*. Todd tells his clients, "You've got to come to grips with the *cause* of your cancer. Because if you keep behaving the same way, the cancer will run you over and take your life." Founder's the same way. It can happen, and happen again, and get progressively worse — until the horse succumbs and dies.

[†]Pollit, lecturer at the International Congress at Geneva (December, 1999). For summary of lecture, see "The Anatomy and Physiology of the Hoof Wall," by Chris Pollit, European Farriers Journal, no. 84, 6/2000.

When I talk with my clients, of course, I discuss the pathology with them, because that's what they see and fear the most. But like Todd, sooner than later, I draw them away from the pathology and into the holistic focus where the "cure" lies waiting. You'll never find it in the pathology, nor in the conventional treatments that are designed to "combat" the founder pathology, rather than treat the cause. It just isn't there.

Consider now that tremendous scientific forces have been brought to bear on founder in the last decade. But as in the war on cancer, the battle is far from being won. Arguably, it is being lost. Morgues and slaughterhouses testify to this, as do the unprecedented numbers of foundered horses visibly stumbling about in the world. As I write these words, one vet I know of, is personally treating over 500 cases of founder in his own area.

Not so on the holistic front of natural cures and prevention. Here, there is no battleground. Just "simple" cures based on simple management changes. Changes in how we relate to and care for our horses. And nothing more.

I suspect that some readers are turned off by two words I've been using, and will continue to use, again and again. These are *natural* and *holistic*. To be quite honest, I can't agree more with their frustration. These two terms have probably been more abused by charlatans and carpet knights than most of us can ever imagine. Their true import has been nearly ruined by commercialism and misapplication of what the terms should stand for in peoples' minds. And it is my opinion that this corruption in meaning might never have happened, had conventional medical and veterinary societies done the right thing from the beginning: absorb these important dimensions of life and healing into their professions and establish protocols for practicing them responsibly.

So far as treating laminitic horses is concerned, I use these terms very specifically. *Natural* refers to what happens in the horse's natural world, exemplified by our wild horses. We cannot deduce what is natural for horses from domestic situations, and for what I hope are obvious reasons to the reader. The mark of humans in domestic horse populations cuts too deep to infer much of anything about genuine naturalness.

By *holistic*, I mean the "whole horse," including all the various forces that influence his being. Hence *holistic care* refers to the treatment and prevention of lameness (e.g., founder) that takes into account the horse's entire life. We look closely at the lifestyle he is compelled to live in captivity, and we suggest changes in management in order to provide more natural care.

Conventional veterinary therapies, in contrast, are principally (if not exclusively) concerned with treating the symptoms of founder pathology (e.g., pain and coffin bone rotation). Few practitioners are interested in advocating or administering to lifestyle changes, since these are seen as ancillary to proper treatment. It is fine to make possible changes in diet, they will argue, but first "coffin bone rotation" must be dealt with. Holistic care, to the extent that it is even acknowledged, is usually viewed as "preventive medicine" by traditional veterinary practitioners. They may scoff at its practitioners, whom they perceive as "wafty wackos" and murky "fringe types." I can't entirely disagree with them though, at least in some instances, because there are many "holistic practitioners" out there who fit that description. They know nothing about wild horses nor are they cognizant of what constitutes genuine natural care. They're more liable to try to "fix" hoof imbalance by setting acupuncture needles in the horse's neck, or by massaging joint muscles of the leg, or by giving the horse some kind of herbal "drench," than simply looking at the hoof to see what needs to be done to it. Of course, if you don't know what a naturally shaped hoof looks like, including how it is "balanced," or how to wield trimming tools to fix the problem, what else can you do except prescribe generalized "alternative" therapies based on the human imperative? That doesn't work, since we're talking about two different species. I caution horse owners not to throw human and equine therapeutic needs into the same pot. Understanding who and what the horse is must be the foundation for any facet of genuine holistic care.

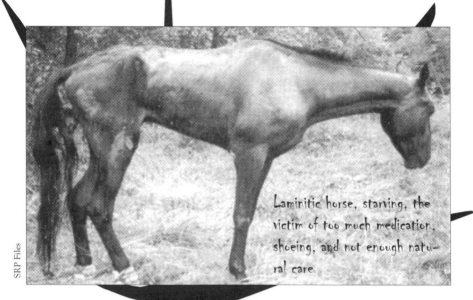

Laminitic horse, starving, the victim of too much medication, shoeing, and not enough natural care.

The author cares for horse suffering from "hoof slough" — the hoof capsule, purulent with infection, oozed off of the coffin bones of all four hooves.

Regardless, for a horse owner dealing with all the trauma con-summate in a foundered horse, it is neither comforting nor en-couraging to hear the vet/farrier castigate the natural or holistic path to healing. This is why it is so important to "clear our minds" and try to understand the causality of founder. To get at the truth, rather than becoming a captive audience to unsubstantiated opin-ions and a victim of voodoo medicine, conventionally or holisti-cally so.

To clear our heads, we need useful information with which to supplant our uncertainty and to act intelligently upon. *A plan of action.* As an experienced holistic hoof care practitioner, I've found it easiest to begin by addressing issues of pathology. Like I said before, this is usually where horse owners are at in their heads. And most need to reason their way out of it before they can begin to act from a holistic perspective. I will also discuss why their pro-fessionals are doing what they're doing, and why it's not working, or not working well or with any consistency.

I'm thinking now back to Todd's store when one of those can-cer victims happened in one day, while I was there. Emaciated, and in obvious pain, the fellow said, "Sir, I've had surgery and ra-diation for my cancer, and I'm sick from all these medications, and I'm dying. Sir, can you help me?" Well, I've received that kind of call not infrequently myself.

About a year ago, a lady called after her son found me during an 11th hour search on the Internet. The very next morning, her vet, who had given up all hope, was coming (by appointment) to eutha-nize her suffering horse. After the usual rounds of conventional treatment had not worked, her horse was in a steady decline. Aided by her son, who found my website, she had reached the very edge of the fringe, as I think of my position relative to conven-tional veterinary and farriery care, and had no where else to turn. It was her last ditch effort, and, yes, that's the way it usually is out here in the fringe. We're positioned at the end of the line. There's no where else to go:

"Mr. Jackson, I'm calling because I found you on the internet, where I was searching to find something that will save my foundered horse. He's in bar-shoes, with pads, and these are the medications he's on. I've been through three farriers and as many vets. None of them agree on what to do. I've spent several thousand dollars, and my horse is in such pain that I can no longer stand to see him suffer. My vet is coming to put him down tomorrow. Sir, I just want to know if there is anything you can do to save him?"

2 War on pathology

Within the hoof, nucleus of the laminitic attack, I see 'P3-rotation' as a cleansing and an opportunity. It is nature's metabolic effort to shed the hoof of pathology — diseased horn arising from dietary toxicity — and pave the way for healing. So, if confronted with the specter of laminitis, it is not my practice to oppose it, through drugs, heart-bar shoes, pads, and other control devices, but instead to invite it into the vast realm of holistic care. And once there, to see it through and assist it in every possible way to its inevitable conclusion: a natural healing. — Jaime Jackson

NEW LAMINITIS EVIDENCE PRESENTED

Speaking at an extended seminar about his research as part of last week's American College of Veterinary Surgeons annual meeting in San Francisco, Dr. Chris Pollitt of the University of Queensland, Australia, presented the results of his latest research into the pathogenesis of laminitis. Pollitt's research identifies the microorganism *Streptococcus bovis* in the equine hind-gut as the culprit in laminitis. S. bovis produces a substance that activates lamellar enzymes (MMP-2) and causes lamellar separation . . . if Pollit can now prove that it can cross the mucosal barrier of the hind-gut and enter the circulation, the real "cause" of carbohydrate-induced laminitis will be harrowed significantly, and, possibly, an inhibiting medication could be developed to prevent laminitis. [Oct./1999, *Hoofcare Online–Hoofcare & Lameness: The Journal of Equine Foot Science*]

I spoke at the same 1995 Bluegrass Laminitis Symposium as Dr. Pollit, both of us guests of veterinarian Dr. Ric Redden, host of this annual event. My presentation was an enactment of what one does to become accepted into a wild horse band — a process necessary to learn from them in their midst, from within their world, rather than as a voyeuristic, part-time outsider and nuisance. I followed with a detailed description of wild horse hooves, my model

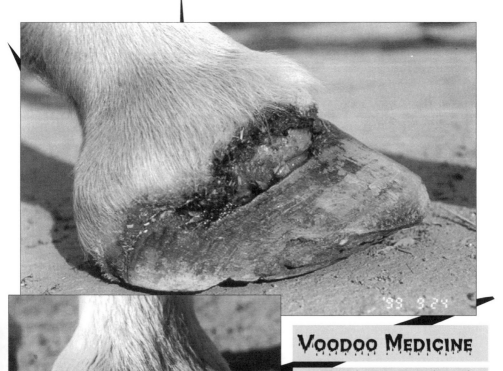

VOODOO MEDICINE

These hooves were subjected to a form of medieval trepanning called "coronary grooving." The results of this barbaric practice can be horrendous. (*Top*) Coronet has prolapsed and opened hoof to infection. (*Left*) Lateral quarter has collapsed along lines of "grooves" which are scored in the outer wall with an electric rotary burr. Independent research, published in the American Farriers Journal in 1999, showed "no clinical improvement of grooved horses over un-grooved horses" receiving conventional veterinary care. (*Bottom*) Notorious heart bar shoe is removed from grooved hooves of Arabian dressage horse in preparation for natural hoof care. [See Natural Hoofcare Advisor, v. 1, no. 5 (Jan/Feb, 2000) for complete story on these photos.]

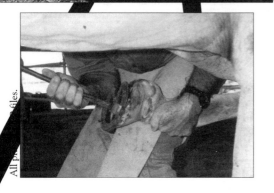

of 20 years for bona fide natural hoof care.

At that time, Pollit was reporting the pathological effects of laminitis on the "basal membrane" — the extra-cellular material forming a partition between the lamina and coffin bone that I discussed in the previous chapter. But five years later, Pollit and his colleagues' attention, witness the above press release, have shifted to a harmful micro-organism (*S. bovis*) believed to be penetrating the horse's gut, and producing secondary agents in the vascular system reaching the laminar membrane of the hoof, where all havoc is wrought by the MMP enzymes.

I guess it is fair to say, Pollit and others have been as busy looking inside the horse's foot, as I have been looking at it from the outside, trying to look at the "whole picture." Their focus has centered around pathology, mine around what is healthy and natural. And I guess that sums up the main, "upfront" difference between "natural" and "conventional" approaches to treating founder.

But if we follow that watershed a bit further, our differences become more pronounced, dramatically so, to say the least. Conventional therapies become battlegrounds — gallant efforts to see who is tougher: man's technology or the pathological forces of founder? Our vets and shoers are not afraid to show their stuff either, witness their arsenals of drugs, surgical procedures, and orthopedic shoes. Nature, however, being what it is, has made sure that the laminitic enemy can fight back just as tenaciously, and for every conventional warhead fired, a bigger bomb is returned in rotated coffin bones, dropped soles, and sloughed hooves. The fight is on!

Now, when the phone rings in my office, a distressed horse owner calling from somewhere out there in America, I get virtually the same run-down on what the vets and shoers (and even some of those "holistic practitioners") have been up to in their fight against founder. There's a little variation from call to call, but not much. Here "at the fringe," most of the horses that reach me are in pretty rough shape, although some horse owners reach us well before their horses arrive "at death's door." Whatever the case, they are trying desperately to locate useful information to help their horses with. "Desperation" is usually the driving human emotion that brings horse owners to the fringe.

Typically, horse owners haven't a clue what to do, or, for that matter, even know what is happening exactly. Few realize that the symptoms of laminitis — pain, inability to move normally, and even the tell-tale "stretched" white line (page 39) often concealed by the farrier's horseshoe — occur long after the causality of the inflammation has done its dirty work.

The war on founder pathology usually commences soon after the horse displays the first symptoms of what veterinary scientists term *laminitis*: an inflammation of the laminar structures described in the previous chapter (see also the photo illustrations on page 81). It is normally accompanied by painful sensitivity. Laminitis usually strikes in both the front and hind feet, however it is symptomatically more pronounced in the front. This is probably due to the fact that the front feet bear more of the horse's weight and because the front hooves are closer to the horse's heart — one wonders what motivates hungry toxins searching for the nearest ripe territory to invade.

The laminitic attack may be accompanied by such relatively minor pain as to suggest only a minor disturbance of the horse's natural gaits, or of such magnitude as to keep him teetering in the archetypal "founder stance" [see Cover illustration] or writhing and moaning flat out on the ground (or up and down, if the poor guy can't find any relief one way or the other). Whatever, the biochemical cause of the laminitis, or tearing of the lamina, precedes the distressing symptoms. But it doesn't really matter, for, like cancer, it's only an issue of how we're going to get rid of it. And nothing less.

What does one do next?

Customarily, horse owners call the vet and shoer, of course. Conventionally, many vets will have the farrier pull the horse's shoes (if he's in keg shoes, and he usually is), and then re-shoe him with special bar shoes or shoes with frog pads. The logic of these orthopedic shoes and pads is to "give support" to the weightbearing coffin bone inside the hoof, which is losing (or has lost) its laminar attachments to the outer wall. No one will argue, indeed, that the bone is breaking loose and will, if something isn't done, start pushing through the sole. The nightmare of this specter is sufficient to motivate most horse owners to get going with the vet's program.

A few vets will forsake the shoeing, temporarily anyway, and tape foam pads to the bottom of the horse's feet. The foam isn't soft like in a sofa or mattress, but firm like packing material used in shipping computers, VCRs, etc. Like bar shoes and pads, the foam provides a direct means of supporting the sole and, above that, the disengaging coffin bone. Likewise, the foam support attempts to shift the horse's weight off of the distressed laminar junctions and onto the sole, frog, shoe, pad, and/or foam.

Underneath all those shoes, pads, and foam, it's often hard to discern how the farrier has actually trimmed the horse's feet. But without even looking, it is a fact that few can agree on how it should be done. The farrier literature demonstrates unequivocally that farriers concur on the point that the hooves will need to be trimmed differently — and all in accordance with the progression of the pathology, the horse's previous treatments, his breed or conformation, hoof "type," how he will be used, and where he will be boarded. The prospect or value of "natural trimming" based on the wild horse hoof model is largely ignored.[†]

Typically, most professionals will try to thin or rocker the toe wall, pointing out, quite correctly, that the hoof is much pained in this area. That by removing as much of the wall around the toe as possible (including resections), weight bearing and locomotive resistance (lever forces) are minimized and, hence, a palliation of sorts is effected in the reduction of pressure induced pain. Some

---

[†]This may be changing. Farriers from around the U.S. have contacted me in the past year to report their successes with the natural trim approach to remodeling the laminitic hoof. The American Farriers Association has published my articles on the subject.

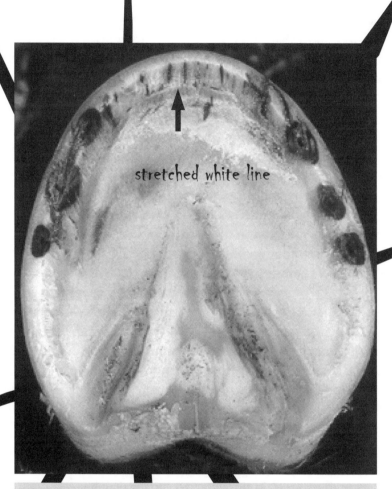

stretched white line

Telltale "stretched" white line of laminitic hoof is revealed after horseshoe is removed. This is but one symptom of laminitis, which with all symptoms discernable to the human eye, including movement dysfunction and pain, occur in the aftermath of founder's causality. Hence, the importance of implementing preventative holistic lifestyle measures.

shoers, including myself at one time, might attempt to achieve a similar effect by nailing a "reverse shoe" on, that is, by nailing a keg shoe on backwards so that the toe of the shoe covers the heel and frogs (like an egg-bar shoe), while the shoe branches extend forward along the quarters, but falling short of the toe. In this position, the toe wall is liberated simultaneously from pressure caused by the shoe and from direct contact with the ground.

Aggressive "4-Pt. Trim" practitioners will go one step further and curette the toe wall and quarters until the entire front third of the hoof's natural bearing surface (i.e., the outer wall) is rendered completely passive to the sole. Taking another path, a particularly aggressive veterinary practitioner may surgically excise a goodly portion of the toe wall as well — called a "resection" — and treat the remaining exposed laminar corium as an open wound; so configured, there is no way for the toe to bear weight!

In a severe laminitic attack, the pain may be so intolerable that the vet must use pain killers before the farrier can get the horse to stand long enough to nail on the orthopedic shoes. In some instances, the horse is shod laying right on the ground, so debilitating is his pain. The same vet may administer other drugs as well to increase circulation, reduce swelling, and lower the hoof's temperature. If the laminitis was triggered by colic, then the vet may dole out other drugs for that too. Dr. Pollit, I understand, is exploring the use of "MMP inhibitor agents" to get at those harmful enzymes I mentioned earlier. This is a treatment process that, Todd points out, Pollit is borrowing from oncologists who use these chemicals in combating cancer in humans. So horses may be looking forward to that too in the not too distant future.

Now think about it. Orthopedic shoeing aside, we're also talking about an awful lot of chemicals for a sick horse to be ingesting and metabolizing. Chemicals which will be moving systemically through the horse's blood stream to the hooves, to that already inflamed laminar corium. Add to these other chemicals the horse may already have in his body — parasiticides, vaccines, feed supplements for the hooves, grain concentrates — and we may have even concocted a new synergized recipe for founder!

And we're not done yet.

The horse, in spite of his misery, is probably still hungry. What are we going to feed him? Nothing? Just hay? What kind of hay? Grain? No grain, some grain, what kind of grain?

And, although he can hardly move, where are we going to keep him? And will we give him complete "bed rest" in a locked stall or will we make him move? Even though he is in such great pain he can barely stand?

If his feet are hot and pulsating, do we lead him somehow to cool water to stand in? Or does he need to stand in warm water as some authorities insist? And speaking of water, can we let him drink cold water? After all, other authorities are convinced that even this can cause laminitis.

Alright, enough! I think we should stop right here and not dwell another moment on any of the specific weapons of the conventional therapies alluded to above. Horse owners who have gravitated to this little book have already heard and seen enough of it. They are after something else, and that's what this book is all about.

So, what do we do exactly to affect the natural cure of founder? Well, we are going to learn to identify and remove the offending causes of founder, and return the horse to a natural lifestyle. Just that, and, other than some specialized and non-invasive hoof work, nothing more.

3 Holistic forces to the rescue

Thus it appears advisable to me to look back from the perfect animal and to inquire by what process it has arisen and grown to maturity, to retrace our steps as it were, from the goal to the starting place, so at last when we can retreat no further, we shall feel assured that we have attained to the principles.
— William Harvey, M.D., *Essays On the Generation of Animals (1651)*

It seems to me that there is no higher technology in the treatment of founder than common sense. — Jaime Jackson

Holistically, our approach to stopping the founder menace will be to line up as many of the kinds of lifestyle conditions we see in wild horse country as possible. This doesn't mean we're going to try to turn our sick horse into a wild horse. Only that we want to give him lifestyle opportunities that are not conducive to founder pathogenesis but which are healthy for horses based on the wild horse model. Which means, as I discovered back in the early 1980s, that in most cases all we have to do is just simplify his life.

In effect, we want to put into place a system of natural management practices, and then invite your horse and his founder into them. The deeper he goes into these holistic changes, the harder it will be for the founder to hold its ground. Indeed, with diligence, it will simply retreat and fade away.

I seldom have to "argue" the merits of holistic care with horse owners who have reached the fringe, that mysterious place, as I think of it, between domestication and wildness (i.e., naturalness). My experience has been they are ready for something that makes sense, which is in fact natural and good for their horses.

So, to get started, I listen attentively to their observations about what has happened up to that point with their horses. Familiar with the founder topography, I'll try to jostle their memories a bit so that I get confirmation of the disease's cause. To help, I always provide horse owners with a consultation form which instructs them to write out what has happened — therapy, diet, boarding ar-

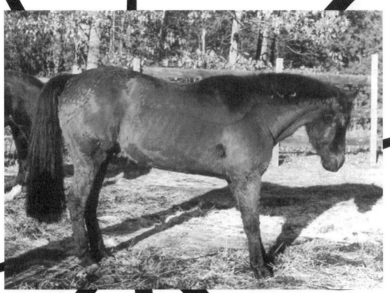

Bar-shod and trapped in the founder stance with no where to go.

rangements, etc. — and which provides me with close-up photographs of the hooves and specific measurement data.

On one level, this approach provides me with clear information about how far the founder pathology has progressed and what's been done about it so far. As a hoof care expert, I can tell a lot from looking at the photos and reading the measurement data. I've even invented a unique hoof gauge, called the Hoof Meter Reader ("HMR"), to help horse owners and professionals measure the hooves in a standardized way. If, however, the horse owner is physically unable or too emotionally stressed to gather this kind of information, I will arrange to have a hoof care practitioner I've trained or trust enough to go do this for them. Usually, this skilled hoof care provider will be necessary anyway to initiate the trim work, particularly if the horse owner's farrier is unreceptive to natural hoof care principles. Farriers typically object to the barefoot approach, rather than the actual trim itself.

The consultation service allows the horse owner to talk out the problem or situation as they perceive it, while enabling me to become a part of the treatment and rehabilitation process. Building trust and confidence is so important at this stage, obviously. At this time, they are often the recipients of very intimidating exhortations from their vets and farriers not to break ranks with their treatments, even if the horse is failing. It's really tough on horse owners to go looking out into the fringe for help, and, just as tough to have to then turn around and try to explain to their vets and farriers that they want to "go natural." They need as much support as possible as they step over the line to get on the natural healing pathway.

Once we've established a rapport based on a mutual understanding of the founder pathology, the background of the horse, and the need for a new direction, we begin at once to take a rather sharp, and usually unexpected, turn in the management of the horse. Such is the nature of the holistic path. I always begin with this statement:

You must believe that a horse — any horse, foundered or

otherwise – can stand and move on his own bare feet.

Now this statement may seem preposterously obvious, but it is a fact that in virtually all conventional veterinary founder therapies, horse owners are told that their horses *must be shod* (or padded) if they are to be successfully treated. De-shoeing a laminitic or full-blown foundered horse is considered antithetical to accepted founder treatment, and, as I've heard a hundred times, inhumane. Nevertheless, a barefooted horse is the fundamental starting point in the holistic treatment of founder. *The shoes must be removed.*

Fortunately, by the time horse owners have reached the fringe, most are more than willing to pull the shoes and liberate their horses' feet. I hear time and again, "It just makes sense." To help, I (and a few of my professional colleagues) have prepared several written works and companion videos to help horse owners understand the precise reasons behind "de-shoeing," as I call it, along with trimming instructions on how to do it responsibly. These are referenced in the Resource section of this book.

With the horse de-shod, the real "bend" of the turn in the holistic path to founder healing is now before us. Here lay the holistic lifestyle changes, along with what we call "de-tox" – removing poisons from the horse's body. This is the tough part for many horse owners, who are often reluctant to change set patterns of care and who cling tenaciously to the "security" of the vet's drugs and other practices they are accustomed to. But, at the fringe, with no where else to go except back to the problematic conventional therapies, including euthanasia, most gallantly go through the changes with their horses.

We in the natural hoof care movement, however, try to make it as easy a transition as possible for the horse owner to make. Obviously, breaking their sense of isolation – that they're in some kind of vacuum dealing with the problem alone – is a top priority. If I don't connect them immediately with a natural hoof care practitioner (as mentioned above), I'll connect them to other horse owners who've traveled the path before them. You can call this a "support group," whatever, but it's a way for distraught horse owners to look ahead with confidence, to talk with others who've gone before them, and maybe even attend one of many natural hoof care seminars now being given across the U.S. [see Resources].

But, at the outset, we're still alone together on the path at this early stage. And we've got to get the horse going into the badly needed holistic changes. Talk and support groups aren't enough. Action is needed. And pronto.

It usually takes about an hour for me to explain what needs to be done. I try to paint a comprehensive picture of what we want to do, and where we're going. This is how we forge an actual plan of action together. Some of the parts I'm pretty firm about, others more compromising. I also remind horse owners that it took time to get the horse into this jam, and that he needs time to get out of it. "We've got time," is one of my most articulated exclamations. This can actually be a relief for some horse owners who are feeling pressured to "do something" immediately (i.e., put the horse out of his suffering).

In most founder cases that reach the fringe, the discussion of holistic changes is necessarily broad and encompassing. That's because founder can disguise itself in different ways. Exploring its "hideouts" together is not only necessary, it's also excellent therapy for the distraught horse owner. It's information that empowers him or her to act decisively, overcome guilt, and ultimately save the horse's life and return him to soundness.

Now, when we speak of natural healing, there's really three dimensions involved. One is mental, and concerns bringing the "causality" of founder into a visible place in the awareness of the horse's owner. Holistically speaking, we must eliminate the mental pitfall that founder has a single cause. If we are to restore, or heal, the laminitic horse, we must look into the many unnatural forces at work in his life. Otherwise, no true or lasting healing occurs, except per chance, and we'll be merely spinning our wheels in place with no measurable or consistent progress in the long term.

The second dimension is purely practical and requires that we physically remove damaged and diseased hoof tissue. This is the job of the hoof care provider.

The third dimension involves the forces of natural healing. This means enabling the horse's own healing mechanisms to go to work for us. It's something we can't do for the horse, except to help by instituting the necessary natural lifestyle changes. Natural healing includes the restoration or regeneration of lamina, bone, nerves (many horses are "nerved" by vets), ligaments and tendons (many horses are given tenotomies to prevent coffin bone rotation), blood circulation (rendered less than optimal by orthopedic shoeing), and a solid hoof capsule capable of enduring 15 to 20 miles of hard riding over moderately difficult terrain without the protection of a horseshoe. Concerning the latter, all laminitic and foundered horses, without exception, should be pain free, sound and rideable at the end of their holistic treatment.

In summary, the three dimensions of natural healing are effected by "naturalizing" the horse's lifeway and giving him genuine natural trims. And nothing more.

Okay, you're probably excited by this good news. So the time has come to roll up your sleeves and get to work. The next six chapters describe the principal areas of holistic change that are likely to be called upon, and we will go through them one by one together. These mainly concern the hooves, the necessity of "natural equine movement," diet, and the elimination of man-made chemicals from the horse's body. They are gauged to expose and root out the usual causes of founder. And to keep them at bay (i.e., prevention) forever. There's nothing complicated about any of this, and what makes the holistic path so unusual — the "bend" so pronounced — really, is its surprising simplicity. At the risk of sounding naive, may I suggest that the holistic healing of founder requires nothing more than the most rudimentary understanding of a horse's basic (i.e., natural) needs and *common sense*:

> Our goal is to aid and abet the horse's marvelous natural healing system, rather than to mechanically manage the symptoms.

4   The hooves themselves

An important cornerstone of lameness treatment in natural hoof care is recognizing that the hoof is basically a sound structure and seldom, if every really, the root cause of serious lameness. The hooves are simply a repository for anti-holistic forces besieging the horse. Thus, one of the cardinal rules of natural or holistic lameness treatments is this: *The hoof cannot be forced to make the horse sound.*
 — Jaime Jackson (*Horse Owners Guide To Natural Hoof Care*)

I've already mentioned the horse's feet, but further clarification is needed if you're new to the natural hoof care movement. Refer to this book's Resources section where you'll find sources for very detailed information about managing your horse's hooves the natural way. For now, our focus will be to remove the horse's shoes (if he's shod) and initiate the natural trimming method, taking into account the special considerations of the laminitic hoof. Let's dive right in.

Importance of removing the shoes

I mentioned in the previous chapter that the horseshoes have to be removed, and that barefootedness is our starting point in natural, holistic hoof care. The reason is that you can't provide genuine natural hoof care with the shoes present. Why?

There are two principal reasons. First, the presence of the shoe prevents natural wear, so the hoof continues to grow longer and longer while creating dangerous lever forces on the inflamed and weakened toe lamina. In contrast, the unshod hoof can wear from natural movement and it can be trimmed as often as needed to sustain a reasonably natural hoof length. This provides your horse's feet with an important biomechanical advantage. And a foundered horse needs every mechanical advantage we can give him to make natural movement possible. *This is the key.*

Second, and very important, an unshod hoof is able to expand

" . . . even the worst can be
returned to their natural shapes"

and contract as the horse moves along. This "flexing" of the hoof is called the *hoof mechanism*. The mechanism is necessary for optimal circulation, and this is what a foundered horse needs most to heal the damaged lamina and generate healthy junctions to the outer wall.

Now, if we roll these two vital facets of natural hoof state into a single statement, we'll have an important cornerstone laid in the natural treatment of founder:

> *Barefootedness and natural movement enable optimal blood circulation through the horse's hooves.*

So, if your horse is still in his shoes, then we want to remove them as soon as possible. If he can stand for it, have your vet or farrier pull the shoes now. Or learn to do it yourself. If his feet are so painful that he can't stand on three to give you the fourth to work on, it is probably best to wait another day or two until the cause of his founder is identified and removed. The inflammation should then abate and render shoe removal more feasible without causing the horse undue suffering. Obviously, if your tormented horse can't give you his feet because they simply hurt too much, you aren't going to be able to pick them up without a fight or casting him on the ground.

Now, some vets will give drugs to make the horse sleepy so he won't fight you, along with pain killers. This is not advisable since your horse is sick and doesn't need any more chemicals in his system. The addition of potentially toxic substances could compound his problems by exacerbating the laminitic inflammation. De-shoeing can probably wait another day. As I've said, *you have time.* And time in conjunction with other changes we're going to make, will probably ease the inflammation so you can pull those shoes.

On the other hand, some horses will cooperate in their pain just to get the shoes off, and I don't blame them. As an experienced (ex-) farrier of 24 years, I can snap a shoe off in less than 10 seconds, and if the horse senses that I'm capable of doing it quickly, he'll probably work with me to get the job done. Most foundered horses can and will put up with the discomfort in that time span, and I may have handlers "prop" the horse up on the opposite side with their own bodies to help balance the horse. A cooperative group of horse owners I know who are doing their own hoof work, and helping others with foundered horses, have actually created a fascinating "sling" device to help support agonizing laminitic horses while their shoes are being removed and during trimming.

Once the shoes are pulled, we've now got a bare hoof in contact with the ground. But because your horse is laminitic, the hooves are inflamed and probably are very painful to him. Ouch! This is normal and natural, and nothing to panic or worry about. Ignore it! Or, if it helps you, feel sympathetic. Just keep him barefooted, whatever you do. Many horses, even perfectly sound ones, coming out of shoes for the first time can be tenderfooted too, and you'd think they were foundered! All will get over this tenderfootedness in due time if you are simply patient. And most, except the very worst, won't need much time, a few days if they're trimmed properly. This added tenderfootedness, the result of de-shoeing, is

something your horse will have to bear, and you mustn't think that his founder condition is worsening for it, or that you're a bad person for making him go through it. The shoeing has been hiding it from you all along. Paradoxically, it's actually making him better, because the hoof mechanism is now at work to catalyze the healing process.

To bute, or not to bute?

Chances are, however, that your horse is being given "bute" (phenylbutazone), because vets nearly always bute foundered horses and because horse owners these days tend to use bute on their horses like they use aspirin on themselves. Many horse owners always seem to have the stuff around, and, though it's illegal, they dispense it even though the vet isn't there to prescribe and authorize it *per issue*. So, your horse may be experiencing some pain relief from the bute, although not necessarily so. It depends on the "potency" of the founder cause, and how active that cause still is.[†]

You've probably discovered though that when the bute wears away, the pain gets worse. If it'll help you relax, keep the horse on the bute as prescribed by the vet, but only temporarily. We'll need to start weaning him off it soon enough though, in conjunction with other holistic changes that will aid in the reduction of inflammation and mitigation of his pain.

Please understand that bute is a "crutch" and there is growing evidence that it causes ulceration of the stomach lining and upsets the natural balance of digestive enzymes in the horse's cecum. Bute can, in my opinion, inhibit healing of the hoof's sensitive lamina by disguising the pain and simultaneously abetting the proliferation of digestive toxins (i.e., one of the causes of the founder) reaching the hoof through the complex network of blood vessels channeling into the laminar corium. Horse owners and vets alike,

---

[†]Which raises the question whether the horse is actually foundered. Some colicky horses behave like they're front feet are foundered as they raise their hind legs up to their bellies to "kick" at their discomfort, and the front feet get wobbly. Not to fret, the holistic changes apply exactly the same to colicky, laminitic, and sound horses!

hence, are lulled into a laxity induced by the palliative effects of this powerful drug, while the pathogens responsible for the founder are still insidiously at work, but now under the drug's guised, protective aegis.[†]

Inflammation, contrary to what you may have read elsewhere or been advised, is normal and healthy during healing. The hoof is trying to tell us to make other changes, which, if dutifully performed, will, as stated, mitigate the inflammation and pain, and render these powerful anti-inflammatory medications with dangerous toxic side-effects unnecessary. So, start thinking about that now, if you haven't already.

Of course, if the bute dosage concentrated in his body is such that the pain is sufficiently masked, then you can probably go ahead and proceed with the de-shoeing and hoof work. In other words, take advantage of the situation. Also, if you have a pond or other body of cool water you can lead your horse into, offer to let him stand in it and soak his aching feet. Standing in water, particularly with a muddy or sandy bottom, is perfectly natural for horses. The soothing, cool water may alleviate some of the stress from the laminitis. It will also soften the hooves for trimming, not a bad idea if his hooves are long, hard and dried out.

Now, if you are determined to use bute, here's how I recommend using it to your advantage: Start with your vet's recommended dosage, one or two tablets per day. This dosage should coincide with the implementation of the holistic changes recommended in the following chapters. In other words, don't bute the horse just to kill the pain. Use it to ease your horse onto the healing pathway. Again, the palliation of pain, per se, offers you no guarantee that healing is taking place.

Next, continue the recommended dosage for three days. On the fourth day, withhold the bute. Now, see how your horse is doing over the next 24 hours without medication. If the pain returns

[†]Possibly this is changing; it's been my observation that many vets, much to their credit, are becoming increasingly leery of bute, and are opting to wean horse's off it as soon as possible.

and there is no improvement, or he stops eating, put him back on the bute for another three days.

Continue the "three days on, one day off" cycle, until he begins to show marked improvement. In other words, his pain is obviously abating, he is able to eat, and he moves easier without the bute. When improvement is obvious, begin lowering the recommended bute dosage with your vet's cooperation. If he shows no significant improvement after several days to a week, then the holistic changes (discussed in following chapters) are not being followed consistently.

Finally, when it is clear that your horse is eating well and walking with reasonable comfort (he may still be sore), cease the bute altogether. If after a week, he shows no deterioration, then you are definitely on the healing pathway. Resume the bute cycle at any point in time you and your vet think he is regressing and needs the comforting edge of this particular medication.

Understanding natural hoof care

For many horse owners, the hooves will represent the most "technical" hurdle to surmount in the holistic path. But do not feel daunted, they're not so complicated that you can't understand everything that needs to be done to them to affect a healing. Understanding the hooves is a stepwise process. Foremost, it's really an issue of being able to "see" what a natural hoof "is" and then learning how to transform your horse's feet into that image or form. That's all there is to it, really. And, it is a very simple process. Every professional or amateur natural hoof care provider has his or her own unique way of shaping and finishing the hooves. To me, it's a simple process that encompasses no more than twenty minutes, if that. Many horse owners are now learning to trim and boot their own horse's feet, a trend inspired by their cognizance of the harmfulness of horseshoeing, the unwillingness of many farriers to cooperate in the natural hoof care effort, and their own determination to become more self-reliant.

Now, in contrast to normal hooves, foundered hooves normally

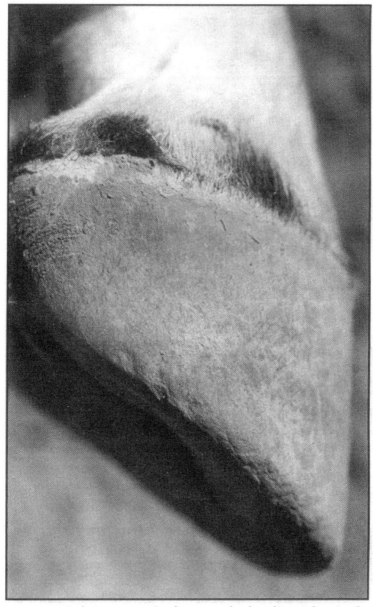

an empowered white mustang hoof . . . perfectly wild and founder free

present a few additional technical challenges in terms of trimming. Laminitic hooves typically deform (witness many of the photos of foundered horses in this book), a propensity easily exacerbated by unnatural trimming methods; indeed, remodeling them can be very confusing if you don't know what you're doing. But not to worry! Even the worst can be returned to its natural shape.

As with any horse that's never had bona fide natural hoof care, foundered hooves should be allowed to transform gradually. A step at a time. We don't need or want to "over-work" the hooves. Over-working the hoof simply adds to the horse's misery by making him tender footed from excessive, close-to-the-quick trimming. Why do this if it isn't necessary? Take a little bit, but more often — say, at three to four week trimming intervals rather than the customary 6 to 8 week intervals most horse owners are accustomed to with shoers — and the horse will transition to soundness much easier. The supporting bone inside the hoof (i.e., the coffin bone) is also going through changes in position, and making gradual changes in the hoof capsule will reduce the stress the shifting bone must endure during healing. I'll discuss these particulars a little further down the path. If you are working with a farrier who is receptive to these ideas, share this information with him or her now.

Initial trim

While the process of doing a natural trim is basically simple, the actual trimming of a foundered hoof, due to the likelihood of temporary deformity of the capsule, is more challenging; hence, it is not something you want to tackle by yourself without training or guidance. I advise also against having your vet or farrier do the trimming, unless they are experienced with trimming hooves for high performance barefootedness or are at least willing to learn. Regretfully, chances of this are rare at this point in time, as the farriery and veterinary industries are very much geared up for founder combat, which means shoeing and pads.

The good news is that you can learn to do the work yourself! And, with practice, you can do it as well as the best professional. Use the Resource section to obtain the necessary learning materials,

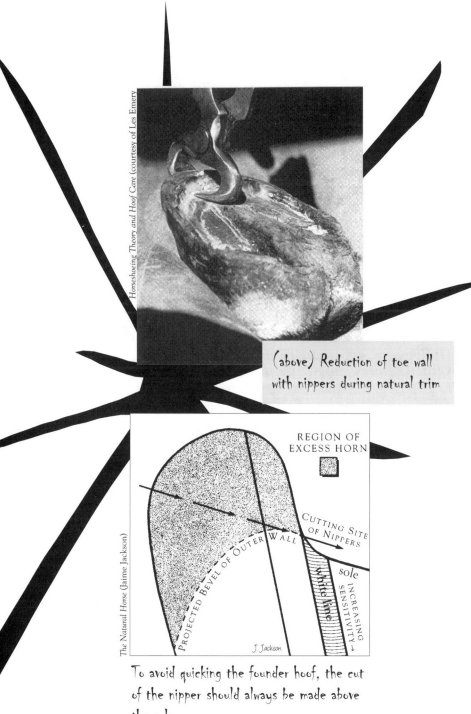

Horseshoeing Theory and Hoof Care (courtesy of Les Emery)

(above) Reduction of toe wall
with nippers during natural trim

REGION OF
EXCESS HORN

CUTTING SITE
OF NIPPERS

PROJECTED BEVEL OF OUTER WALL

White line

sole

INCREASING
SENSITIVITY →

The Natural Horse (Jaime Jackson)

J. Jackson

To avoid quicking the founder hoof, the cut
of the nipper should always be made above
the sole

tools and equipment, and connections to professional natural hoof care providers who can teach you. Whatever you do, don't let anyone trim your horse's feet who doesn't have any idea of the trimming particulars involved. This is an invitation to trouble you may regret. If the trimmer can't produce clients riding barefooted horses, that's probably a strong indicator that they're not qualified to do the job.

For our purposes here, I'll just cover the basics of what needs to be done without overwhelming you with a tissue level discussion of where to place the hoof nippers, knife, and rasp. If your farrier is supportive of the natural approach, then review the following guidelines together:

☑ I recommend that you trim the hind hooves first. But trim them only if they are *very* excessively long, that is more than 3¾ inches from the hairline down the toe wall to the ground (use my HMR, which will give you a standardized reading, to assess this). Make sure the heels are also trimmed naturally short. Trimming the hind hooves first will make it easier for him to "sit back" on his hindquarters, as in the "founder stance," and take weight off his tender forefeet so you can work on them. He'll move easier too, in the future. As with the fronts, the hinds can be gradually brought into a more natural shape. Trimming the hooves gradually, as with making all holistic changes, will simply be easier on him in the long term.

☑ As a general rule, aim to lower the heels to the "periople." The periople is a specialized horn that covers the outer wall just below the hairline. The heels (not the toe) must be trimmed (again, only by a person trained to do this) to approach the periople. Few horses today are trimmed this way by farriers (or vets), because, among other things, they lack specialized training and intricate knowledge of how naturally worn hooves arise from such trimming. It is important to understand that in virtually all cases, natural wear must accompany the trimming process over a period of months before the periople can be reached; in other words, trimming alone

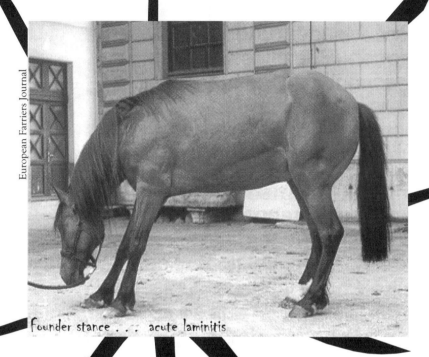

Founder stance . . . acute laminitis

can't do it without quicking the hoof or rendering the adjacent sole hypersensitive. The hooves must be naturally worn — thus the significance of horses going barefooted to acquire truly naturally shaped hooves.

☑ Trim the toe to a reasonably natural length. The length of the toe is a technical issue and must be gauged correctly by someone with experience. My advice is to use the Hoof Meter Reader (HMR) and refer to my trimming book and companion video, available in the Resource section, if you lack experience or are uncertain. Generally, most naturally worn hooves among domestic horses can be trimmed to approximately 3 to 3¼ inches down the toe wall from the coronet. A foundered horse with a dropped sole or disengaged toe wall (severe P3 rotation) will probably take months of trimming to enter this range. Again, much will depend on the degree of foundering that has taken place. If he is in the early stages of acute laminitis, and P3 rotation is minimal or non-existent, then natural toe reduction shouldn't be a problem.[†]

☑ Be respectful and accommodating of the horse's "founder stance." The founder stance [page 59] is a natural posture the horse assumes to relieve pain and promote healing. As the horse "sits back" on the heels of his front hooves, aided by his hind legs, which try to shore up body weight displaced rearward, pressure is removed from the inflamed toe lamina and put over the back half of the front hoof (ostensibly, the objective of caudle support orthopedic shoes and foam support systems). This action tilts the tip of the cof-

---

[†]Wild horses, for your information, are another matter, and I have measured 1400 lb. stallions at 2½ to 2¾ inches down the toe wall! My dissections of wild horse hooves show that the coffin bone appears to assume a higher position in the hoof capsule than in domestic horses. Its neck also appears to be surrounded by more fibro-fatty substances, suggesting a "cushioning" effect. My feeling is that this arises from variations in the degree of wear, rather than genetic differences between wild and domestic equids. Which is to say, that through shoeing and idleness, we have coddled the domestic horse's feet into a weakened parody of its wild cousin. It is unlikely that your horse's hooves can be trimmed this close.

fin bone upward slightly, enough anyway to reduce lever forces adversely impacting the inflamed toe lamina. At the same time, this tilting, often accompanied by a shift of body weight from left to right, increases heel pressure and amplifies the hoof mechanism. So don't be alarmed by this behavior, which encourages blood to enter the hoof's various growth coriums: coronary, laminar, sole, frog/bulbs, and perioplic. He's doing it for a good reason. It's part of the natural healing pathway. We can help the horse engage the founder stance by keeping the toes and heels naturally short.

☑ After the hinds are done, trim the fronts, paying equal attention to natural toe and heel lengths. Again, refer to the Resource section to reference the books, instructional videos, and connections to professional natural hoof care providers. You'll need these in order to learn how to properly trim your horse for barefootedness. This little book is not a "how to" hoof care book, but a "why" and "plan of action" guide.

Summary

When the initial "natural trim" is finished, your horse will be immediately set on the path to natural healing. Unfortunately, there is a good possibility that you will run into much resistance and criticism from your vet and shoer for taking this approach, and possibly from fellow horse owners too. They will tell you that in removing his shoes, you will do him no good, and probably cause him considerable harm. To stand strong against this type of criticism, you must understand why barefootedness is important and how it works. Then you will be able to explain to them why it isn't harmful, and why it's the best treatment path possible to take.

To arm you personally against this potential wall of intimidating resistance, we need to address some of the more common hoof healing concerns you're likely to face. Understanding these concerns within the context of natural healing will free you from the widespread founder paranoia that victimizes and paralyzes so many horse owners. As Todd would say, they will help to "keep a clear mind."

5 Hoof healing concerns

Immobility and crippling result if the connection between hoof and bone (the lamellar distal phalangeal attachment apparatus) fails. Considerable selection pressure against such failure (otherwise known as laminitis) must exist among wild equids, as a foundered animal would quickly attract the attention of predators. — Dr. Chris Pollit (International Congress on Laminitis, Geneva, Switzerland, 1999)

In fact, to trim a hoof for barefootedness based on the principles of modern blacksmithing is to invite a complete disaster for the horse. There is nothing in common between blacksmithing and natural hoof care, except the horse and its hooves awaiting care. The reader is urged to forget about horseshoeing standards and methods altogether. They do not apply. — Jaime Jackson (*Horse Owners Guide To Natural Hoof Care*)

Natural healing of foundered hooves encompasses some very important biomechanical, physiological, and structural adaptations of the hooves. These concern the impact of barefootedness relative to coffin bone rotation, the emergence of a new hoof capsule from within the old foundered one, restoration of the sole's natural concavity, and the optimizing of blood flow through the hoof's vascular system. My experience has been that these issues are usually neither understood nor appreciated by conventional veterinary and farriery practitioners — due largely to the fact that vet and farrier schools teach pathology rather than soundness. In fact, vets and farriers normally compromise them by their unnatural hoof care practices. So, it's incumbent upon you as the horse's owner to understand them and see to it that they are not impeded by unnatural hoof care methods. Let's discuss these now, since you will want to see them through with your own horse.

Barefootedness (and "fear of P3-rotation")

What I really want to address first are the fears horse owners

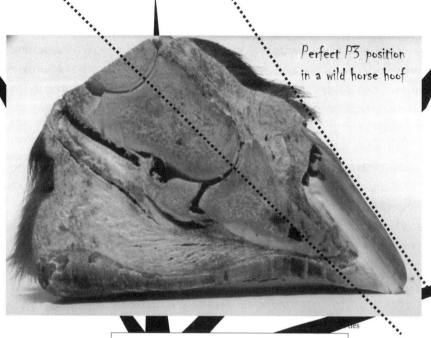

Perfect P3 position in a wild horse hoof

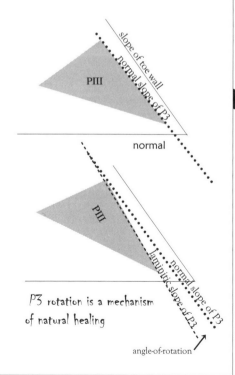

slope of toe wall

normal slope of P3

PIII

normal

PIII

normal slope of P3

laminitic slope of P3

P3 rotation is a mechanism of natural healing

angle-of-rotation

like yourself are probably harboring about a foundered horse going barefooted. The most dreaded fear, of course, is the one that inspires vets and farriers to put on those bar shoes with pads, or the foam support "systems", in the first place. Namely, "coffin bone rotation," or "P3 rotation" for short.

Rotation is a term I actually loathe and wish had never been coined. The "ring" of the word almost implies a rather mechanical if not abiotic "maneuver" within the capsule. Which is hardly the case, from a holistic perspective. Conventionally, rotation is defined as a change, measurable in degrees, in the position of the coffin bone with respect to the toe wall of the hoof capsule. The front of the coffin bone loses its normal position in the capsule as it tears away from its laminar junctions and descends towards (and even into or through) the sole. Hence the expression, "rotation."

The degree, or angle, of rotation is a measurement of how far the front of the coffin bone "rotates" away from an axis parallel to the dorsal (front) surface of the toe wall. This is illustrated on page 63. The greater the degrees of change, the greater the angle-of-rotation. And the greater degree of horse owner fear too.

Accordingly, conventional veterinary therapists are very adamant that the bone must be given ancillary orthopedic "support" to prevent this occurrence. And they are quick to whip out "rotation radiographs" with which to impress and warn unwitting horse owners. One hears, variously, your horse has 3 degrees of rotation, or 5, or 8, and on up. On the advice of some veterinary expert, one popular horse magazine recently went so far as to proclaim an "outer limit" of 10 degrees rotation, beyond which, the article asserts, horses will die. (Consultation clients of mine report as much as 19 degrees of rotation on horses still living!)

But, all of this "fear of rotation" overlooks a very important fact, one which in fact lies at the bottom of natural healing :

> *Rotation in all hooves is a perfectly natural and normal mechanism by which the coffin bone alters its position inside the hoof capsule. Thus, rotation is consistent with natural healing.*

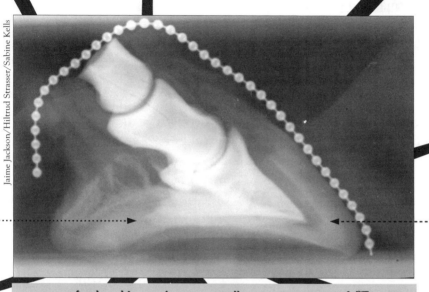

Jaime Jackson/Hiltrud Strasser/Sabine Kells

perfectly wild — the anatomically correct position of P3

= ground-parallel basal alignment of coffin bone

As stated, this re-orientation ("rotation") of the coffin bone goes on in all horses at any given time a change in angle-of-growth is needed to re-balance the hoof. In other words, it's an adaptive mechanism. It only becomes pathological when we founder the horse. Even so, natural hoof care providers still view rotation as a normal and healthy response (albeit an extreme one) by the hoof to abnormal and unhealthy lifestyle conditions imposed upon the horse, which express themselves laminitically. Consequently, rotation is something I never fear, but instead work with to effect healing.

Now, I don't mean to imply that laminitic rotation is a happy event. Nature, I'm sure, has intended it to occur in much smaller increments than is seen in laminitis. Indeed, the greater the degree of rotation, the harder it's going to be on the horse. But this is to be expected. The horse's life, and probably his hooves, are simply too out of whack. Too far out of balance. "Too unnatural." And Nature is fully capable of "rotating" that hoof right off the horse if we fail to get the message and do something about our gross negligence. We must give back to the horse the kind of lifestyle *he needs* to be a real horse. That is how I "read" Nature's founder warning, "coffin bone rotation."

To understand why rotation isn't our enemy, that is, an event we want to resist with shoes, pads, foam, and so forth, we have to look inside the hoof to see what Nature is trying to achieve from a holistic healing standpoint. So, let's look!

"Hoof within a hoof" (fear of the "double hoof")

Foremost, we must recognize that, like your own nails, the hoof is always growing outward from its various coriums: the outer wall from the coronary corium, the lamina from the laminar corium, the sole from the solar corium, the frog and heel-bulbs from their corium. It does this perpetually so — generating healthy new horn to replace the old, which, ultimately, is lost to wear. This equilibrium occurs at a genetically driven rate of approximately 1 cm per month. Which is to say, the hoof is capable of regenerating itself "from within" at an orderly rate of about 10 percent of its total mass every 30 days.

This fact, which may come as a pleasant surprise to the reader, is the actual basis for natural healing. What I mean is that, once we identify and remove the founder cause, and get the horse through the ordeal of founder's acute phase, we can regenerate a whole new hoof within about 9 months while the old pathological capsule is removed from normal wear aided by genuine natural trimming. And there's more good news, many foundered horses should "sound out" within 3 to 4 months, and I mean become rideable in that time. The very worst may require up to a year on the healing pathway to attain pain-free soundness.

Now, as this new growth emanates from the different hoof coriums, the coffin bone is no idle passenger. Rotated out of place by the founder, if you will, the regeneration of healthy horn by the growth coriums is constantly trying to situate it into a new place. The object of natural hoof care, of course, is to enable the hoof's regenerative powers to put it where it really belongs. Seldom will that mean going back to where it originally was before the laminitic attack. That's because the hoof was probably not very naturally shaped to begin with. An unnaturally shaped hoof wreaks havoc with an anatomically correct coffin bone position. That many farriers and vets are hell bent on trying to suppress coffin bone rotation, or worse, "de-rotate" badly pre-positioned coffin bones to their pre-laminitic configurations, makes me shudder more than the acute founder attack itself. Spelling no lasting relief for the horse, such efforts are tantamount to sweeping dirt under a carpet. Indeed:

> The natural trim, and time, and instituting a natural lifestyle, provide the true antidote to P3 rotation.

Continuing, an interesting phenomenon will begin to unfold during natural healing as the "new growth" supplants the older, laminitic horn. This is something to be on the look out for, because it's a definite sign of healing. As a new bed of healthy, keratinized ("nail like") laminar horn is laid by the basal cells of the laminar corium below the hairline (– you can't see it because it's out of sight, behind the outer hoof wall), a corresponding new ring-like section of outer wall (which you can see), spawned by the coronary corium, grows down attached to it. I call it the "hoof within a hoof" mechanism of natural healing (facing page).

In effect, what is happening is that your horse is *shedding* his old, laminitic hoof for a new one. The new one appears to emerge right out of the old one, not unlike a snake or tarantula in the process of molting his skin. Don't be alarmed by this development.

Further, you will notice about a month after the laminitic attack has been checked (by holistic lifestyle changes), that the new growth (the aforementioned "ring") below the coronary band is coming in at a steeper angle than the hoof wall below it, particularly at the toe [facing page]. This "angle differential" will continue to be visible as new growth emerges. This is the "healing" angle-of-rotation in natural hoof care. Eventually, after 6 to 9 months, and providing regular trims are conducted at 3 to 4 week intervals, the band of old growth near the bearing surface of the hoof will become narrower and narrower. And finally it will disappear as the last of it is trimmed and worn away. A beautiful new hoof will have emerged in its place, providing, of course, you have faithfully executed and sustained the other holistic measures I'm about to discuss in following chapters.

A "rising dome" (fear of the "dropped sole")

I've discussed so far "rotation" and "hoof within a hoof," two important issues to understand in our natural healing pathway. Now I want to discuss a third change happening in the hoof, which I call the "rising dome" phenomenon. This refers to the restoration of the hoof's natural solar concavity, which is often lost during founder.

The rising dome is perhaps best appreciated in the context of

SRP Files

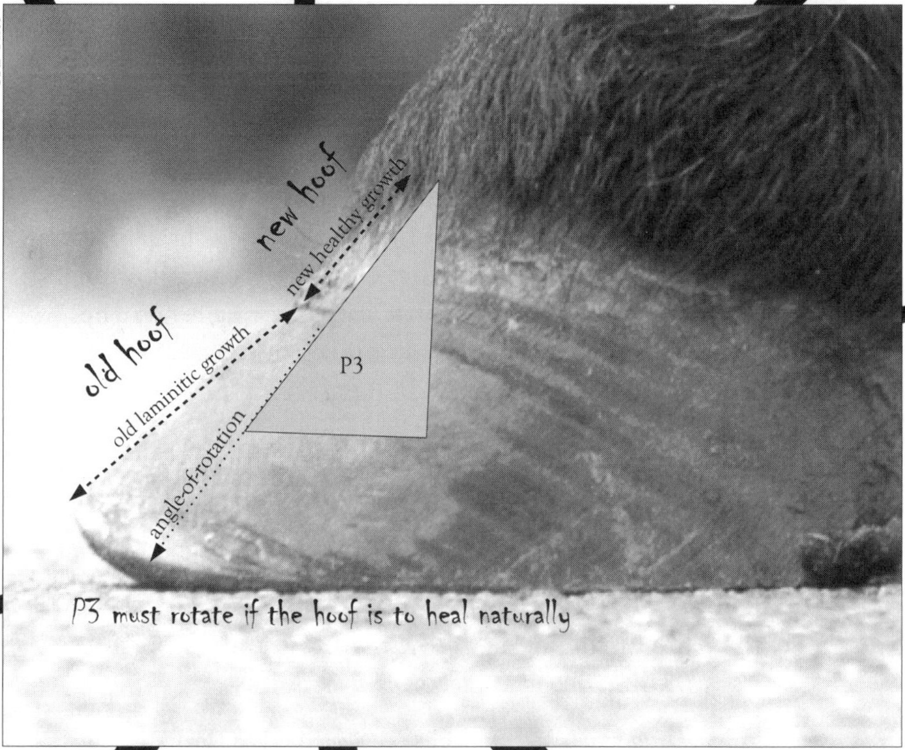
new hoof
new healthy growth
old hoof
old laminitic growth
P3
angle-of-rotation
P3 must rotate if the hoof is to heal naturally

"Hoof within a hoof"

severe rotation. I mentioned earlier that in many founder cases, particularly the worse (which failed to have any holistic intervention), the tip of the coffin bone inside the capsule will jab into the sole and even penetrate it. If you pick up such a foundered hoof and look at the sole roughly midway between the point-of-frog and the center of the toe wall, you'll see either a "hump" (often, a small rise of slightly reddened horn), or, the tip of the coffin bone protruding through the sole. In more advanced founder cases, the entire sole may have simply "flattened out," called a *dropped sole*. In each of these cases, rotation has gotten out of hand.

But it's not the end of the world, and if such is the case with your horse, don't worry about it unnecessarily. Natural healing takes care of this too. For now, I just want to explain how the "rising dome" mechanism occurs — biomechanically, how the sole "gets back up" where it belongs, ridding itself of that dropped sole. Let's do that now . . .

I mentioned that as we remove the founder cause, the laminar corium is able to regenerate healthy new laminar junctions with the outer wall. I mentioned also that these junctions are produced first and closest to the coronary corium, yielding, as discussed above, the band or ring of new growth around the "neck" of the hoof ("hoof within a hoof"). According to Pollit:

> Proliferating lamellar basal cells are confined to the proximal 10% of the lamellar inner hoof wall and are absent in the rest. Thus, in the same way as the hoof wall proper is subject to a downward force exerted by the proliferating basal cell layer of the coronary groove so to are the lamellae. The primary function of the lamellar hoof is to suspend the distal phalanx [coffin bone] within the hoof capsule. It reserves its proliferative potential for the healing of injuries. [Pollit, EFJ (#84)]

Indeed, natural hoof care providers have long recognized this "proliferative potential" of the lamina below the hairline and count on it to heal laminitic hooves in the barefoot state. As Pollit states, the function of the "lamellar hoof" is to "suspend the distal phalanx"; and this precisely is the mechanism we count on to raise the flattened sole into its normal dome-like conformation. An important indicator that the necessary holistic changes in lifestyle are not taking place, is that the hoof's solar concavity cannot be restored through natural trimming. Now, let's see how this works in practical terms.

Assuming we've trimmed the hooves according to natural principles (not difficult!), the base of the coffin bone will assume a new orientation in the capsule. Specifically, we call this the "ground parallel" position of the coffin bone, inasmuch as the base of the coffin bone, which roughly resembles the base of a cone, aligns parallel with the ground. The radiograph in the sidebar (page 65) shows this basal alignment of P3 in a perfectly sound wild horse hoof.

This ground-parallel orientation of the coffin bone is precisely the position that the horse is instinctively attempting to maneuver the bone into when he assumes the "founder stance." So positioned, the inflamed toe lamina are in some measure relieved of painful lever forces. There's not much else the horse can do to try to help himself. But it's an important clue to natural healing. And we natural hoof care providers take it extremely seriously.

In the founder stance, aided by natural trimming, the conically shaped coffin bone is temporarily balanced and stabilized upon its base. As a consequence, the potential for production of healthy laminar attachments (instead of wound serum — characteristic of laminitis) upon its proximal (upper) dorsal surface is now rendered propitious. Presuming this mechanical shift is attended by the necessary holistic lifestyle changes, new laminar attachments will be laid immediately. Within days, newly bonded, keratinized hoof wall will emerge visibly below the coronary band.

Simultaneously, the base of the old, laminitic hoof capsule, itself now re-balanced by natural trimming, provides a support structure — like a belfry suspending a bell — for the new generation of laminar attachments welding the neck of the replacement capsule to that of P3. In effect, we are witnessing a re-suspending of the coffin bone within a new, regenerating hoof capsule. Indeed, that such powerful healing forces exist, even in the most devastating of laminitic cases, is one of nature's great miracles. Once more, Pollit:

> Connective tissue and keratinocytes are now known to remodel and continually upgrade their spatial organization by the tightly controlled production of a specific class of enzymes known as matrix metalloproteinases (MMP-2 and MMP-9). Secreted as inactive proenzymes and, when activated, promptly inhibited by locally produced inhibitors, it is MMP activity which is likely responsible for the remodeling of the various classes of epidermal cells between the basement membrane . . . and the [lamina] . . . After wounding, surviving keratinocytes, responding to locally produced cytokines detach from the basement membrane and commence the re-epithelialization process. [Pollit, EFJ (#84)]

Much of the necessary enzymatic processes driving the re-epithelialization necessary for healing must come from holistic changes outside the hoof. Otherwise, in the words of Pollit, "the triggering of activation of uncontrolled, excessive MMP production" associated with laminitis cannot be regulated — and the hoof will not heal.

Nevertheless, it is clear that the holistic lifestyle changes must be aided by natural trimming and barefootedness. So trimmed, the hoof mechanism (discussed below), rendered optimal by barefootedness, can nourish the coriums with tissue-healing blood, while the hoof capsule once more becomes a secure, stable "housing" with which to suspend the coffin bone. Suspended thusly, the base of the coffin bone is quite literally held up off the ground — the prelude to restoring the hoof's natural concavity. And guess what? That's exactly what happens. The sole goes up right along with the re-suspended base of P3 [facing page]! Conversely, restoring the hoof's concavity, in turn, renders the capsule more flexural and capable of enduring descending body weight, which, in turn, generates a more powerful mechanism. And so

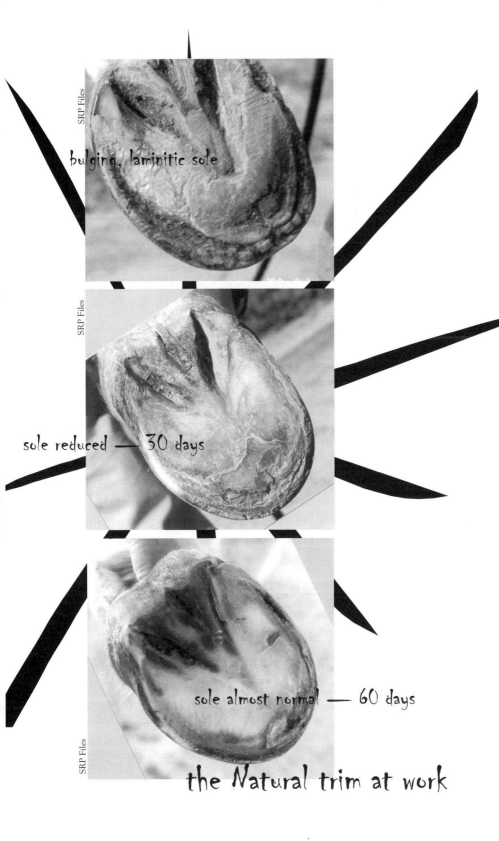

bulging, laminitic sole

sole reduced — 30 days

sole almost normal — 60 days

the Natural trim at work

forth, all things working together as Nature intended.

This inherent healing mechanism of the hoof, aided by frequent physiologically correct trimming, is thus the biomechanical "key" to restoring the sole's natural position and concavity. Hence, the "rising dome" phenomenon, as I think of it.

Having said this, horse owners swayed to this understanding should prepare themselves for massive protests from their more conventional-minded vets and shoers. They will insist that the dropped sole must be forced or "held" in position to prevent P3 penetration. I am reminded of a recent example of this mentality from an article published last year in Europe by the laminitis research group, Budras, Huskamp, Buda, and Petzold. I am mentioning them here because researchers like these are influencing our veterinary community to carry out their misguided therapy recommendations. No doubt the horses of many readers have already been affected by them. According to Budras et al.:

> Chronic, weight-induced laminitis with slight to moderate rotation of P3 implies an increase in blood circulation disorders and therefore necrosis of the old tissue followed by the growth of a second P3 support mechanism. The necrosis process occurring through the old support mechanism, damages the function of the new P3 support mechanism, leading to a drop in P3 and consequently to its rotation . . . .

They add:

> The definitive repair bonding tissue between the new and the old p3 support mechanism is still completely insufficient, because it is produced by horn tubules that are deprived of keratin and also because the new bonding agent is unable to stop the successive tearing related to the dropping of P3 that is gradually getting worse, phenomena due to an increase in overloading . . .
> . . . [These] acute affects of laminitis again destroy a large part of the new P3 support mechanism . . . which due to the destruction of the regenerative potential hinders any positive pro-

European Farriers Journal

before

after

Trimming method advocated by European veterinary researchers (Budras, et al.) is, with drastically shortened heels, close to being natural. But it is ultimately marred by groove cut in toe wall below hairline, by gutted toe wall aimed at displacing weightbearing from the toe on to the sole, and by nailing on a shoe — three unnecessary and potentially dangerous steps.

gress of the patient, in spite of the appropriate therapy, strongly reducing the chances of a cure.[†]

Predictably, the authors recommended treatment is to "temporarily [displace] the weight bearing to the sole, the frog and the heels," using a "prophylactic shoe" designed for this purpose. In terms of actual trimming, they state that "the orthopedic treatment should aim to relieve weight to the parts of the hoof bearing too much weight, cutting a groove in the hoof [toe] wall." [page 75]. Such advice is preposterous and is tantamount to saying, "Natures attempts to heal itself are only making the situation worse." Natural systems, to the contrary, are designed to heal themselves, not self-destruct.

All I can say is hold your ground and resist their conventions, which fail to address two fundamental premises of natural hoof care: 1) The inherent healing capacity of a naturally trimmed hoof to do exactly what they claim it won't, and 2) The synergistic healing influences of related holistic care (e.g., diet), which are nowhere mentioned in their research.

The natural healing ahead will depend on your perseverance and loyalty to the natural healing program, and by not yielding from ignorance or fear to the terrorism of bad science.

Hoof Mechanism

I mentioned "heel pressure" earlier in conjunction with the founder stance and the hoof mechanism. By lowering (i.e., shortening) the heels, and the toe, and thereby simulating the founder stance, the hoof can more readily "expand" under the descending weight of the horse. Hoof expansion, followed by contraction (the

---

[†]K. Budras, S. Buda, B. Huskamp, S. Petzold, "Weight-Induced Comparative Studies With Systemic Laminitis," European Farriers Journal, no. 81, 12/1999.
    They write further, "Prognosis for a complete cure can be possible only in cases where an optimal drug and orthopedic-based therapy is applied. Full recovery of the hoof mechanism can only be hoped for if there has not been significant rotation of the coffin bone." Nonsense!

hoof "shrinks" as it enters its non-weightbearing "flight phase") is a mechanical process that we call the *hoof mechanism.*

The "mechanism," for short, is essential for shock absorbency, traction, and, very important to our discussion of founder, optimal circulation of blood throughout the hoof. Blood — uncontaminated with veterinary chemicals, unhealthy feeds or additives, or diet-induced pathogens — is needed to produce healthy new laminar attachments. The mechanism is a natural "blood pump" for achieving this. As the hoof expands under the weight of the horse, nutrient-rich blood traveling from the heart is literally "sucked" into the growth coriums, where new horn is subsequently produced by basal cells. As the hoof is unloaded during its flight, or non-weightbearing, phase, nutrient-deficient blood is then pumped out of the hoof and back up to the heart. This pumping action is, therefore, instrumental in the replacement of the damaged laminar attachments with new, healthy keratinized laminar horn. A diagrammatic rendering of the mechanism is provided on pages 78 and 79. (Please take a few minutes to study this extremely important information, following it like a road map.)

During laminitis, however, production of healthy lamellar horn is compromised as the basal membrane falls into disarray due to excessive MMP proliferation. The lamina, normally nourished with blood by capillaries emanating from the dermis — which is separated from the laminar basal cells by the membrane — are now deprived; they subsequently swell from inflammation and exude a wound serum [page 81]. Necrosis follows and the laminar attachments to the hoof wall distend and dissociate. P3 rotation then begins. Once this happens, there's nothing you can do about it; moreover, evidence from Pollit seems reliable that the nascent groundwork necessary for laminitic separation commences long before the symptoms become available to the naked eye. Hence, let

(overleaf) The "hoof mechanism"

The "hoof mechanism"

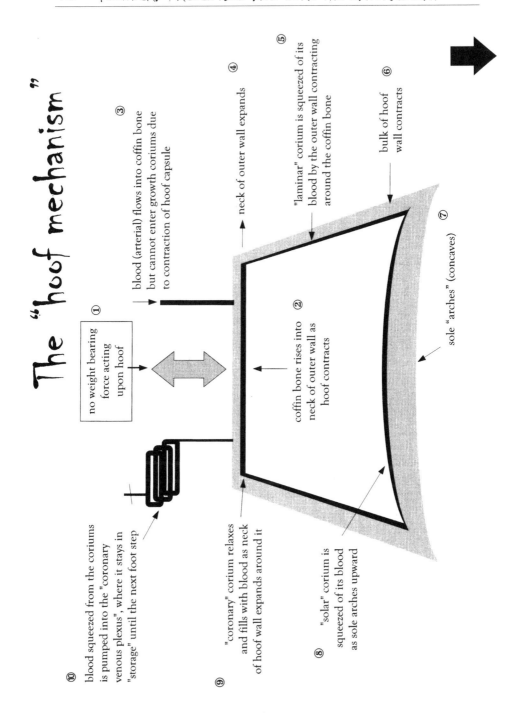

① no weight bearing force acting upon hoof

② coffin bone rises into neck of outer wall as hoof contracts

③ blood (arterial) flows into coffin bone but cannot enter growth coriums due to contraction of hoof capsule

④ neck of outer wall expands

⑤ "laminar" corium is squeezed of its blood by the outer wall contracting around the coffin bone

⑥ bulk of hoof wall contracts

⑦ sole "arches" (concaves)

⑧ "solar" corium is squeezed of its blood as sole arches upward

⑨ "coronary" corium relaxes and fills with blood as neck of hoof wall expands around it

⑩ blood squeezed from the coriums is pumped into the "coronary venous plexus", where it stays in "storage" until the next foot step

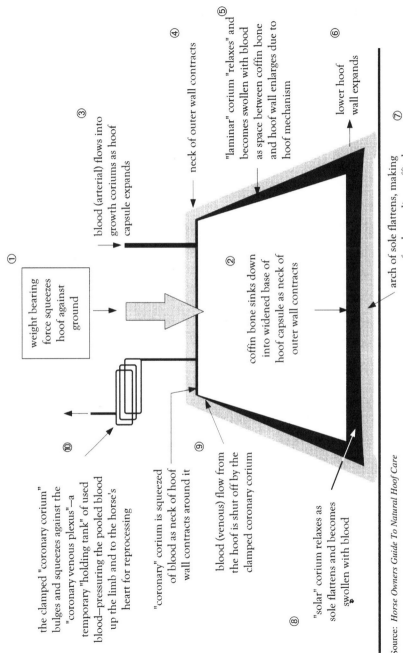

① weight bearing force squeezes hoof against ground

③ blood (arterial) flows into growth coriums as hoof capsule expands

④ neck of outer wall contracts

⑤ "laminar" corium "relaxes" and becomes swollen with blood as space between coffin bone and hoof wall enlarges due to hoof mechanism

⑥ lower hoof wall expands

② coffin bone sinks down into widened base of hoof capsule as neck of outer wall contracts

⑦ arch of sole flattens, making room for descending coffin bone

⑩ the clamped "coronary corium" bulges and squeezes against the "coronary venous plexus"—a temporary "holding tank" of used blood—pressuring the pooled blood up the limb and to the horse's heart for reprocessing

⑨ "coronary" corium is squeezed of blood as neck of hoof wall contracts around it

blood (venous) flow from the hoof is shut off by the clamped coronary corium

⑧ "solar" corium relaxes as sole flattens and becomes swollen with blood

Source: *Horse Owners Guide To Natural Hoof Care*

them die, and concentrate on the holistic front to produce new, healthy growth.

Regrettably, the capillary shutdown is reason enough for many vets in the field to administer vasodilator and anti-coagulant (blood thinning) medications in hopes of *forcing* the constricted arterioles feeding the lamina to open up and allow blood to shunt through. But, vasoconstriction and poor blood flow are not the problem — otherwise, natural healing, and normal repair of injured lamina (not caused by laminitis) would not occur. Indeed, horse's unable to escape the dietary source of their laminitis, will, for no other reason, stand in cold water to bring relief to their aching feet — a form of vasoconstriction. This is nature's way of clamping down on contaminated blood flow while desensitizing the hoof to the pain associated with inflammation.

Clearly, by ignoring the cause (pathological enzymes eroding the junctions themselves, diet, etc.), it is a futile effort to force the hoof to do anything. All that is accomplished is more stress and foreign chemicals in the horse's feet/body. We are merely attempting to address symptoms without treating the cause. The drug is soon shunted away from the laminar corium by arteriovenous anastomosis to other regions of the hoof [page 83] and ultimately into the venous channels leading back to the heart, whence it is recycled throughout the horse's body and back to the feet. A vicious systemic cycle ensues, one which probably compounds further the proliferation of harmful enzymes in the horse's already stressed out hooves.

So here's my point: the inflamed lamina are shut down for a good reason and the cause must be negotiated and removed. Masking the inflammation with anti-inflammatory medications while trying to manipulate the viscosity of the horse's blood, meanwhile ignoring the cause, is strictly a palliative stop-gap. It's not good medicine. And it doesn't work. The underlying cause must be disabled.

For this reason natural hoof care providers instead opt to seek out the cause of the inflammation and remove it at its source. We

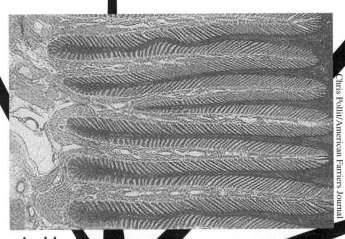

lamina healthy

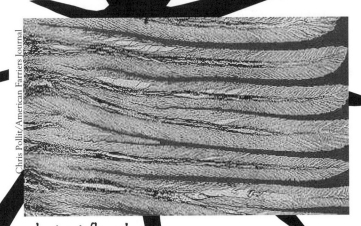

lamina inflamed

know that the hoof mechanism will eventually provide the necessary blood to heal the hoof, but it can't so long as the cause is ignored. We must look beyond the hoof. This seemingly brazen move — to de-shoe the hoof without medications, to give it a natural trim, and then leave it altogether to seek the holistic cure — is currently diametrically opposed to all conventional founder treatments which pitch battle vis-à-vis the pathology at the hoof. Only a few horse owners, accompanied by even fewer vets and farriers, are daring or distraught enough to reach the fringe, and there embrace the powerful holistic forces awaiting them outside the hoof.

Hoof Slough

Ninety nine percent of founder cases can be handled by the foregoing natural trimming strategy. But what if your horse's hooves have fallen completely off — or are about to fall off — as a result of massive inflammation or infection of the laminar corium? In other words, there is no hoof wall left for the horse to stand upon, or to trim for that matter?

This extreme condition of laminitis, known as hoof slough, will require a modified approach. Be aware, however, that most vets will insist that when this stage is reached, there is nothing more that can be done for the horse and it is time to euthanize him. Presuming that you are willing to carry out the holistic changes advocated in the following chapters, then there is no reason to euthanize your horse. To the contrary, your horse should be ready to gallop within a year following the slough. If your vet is willing to work with you on this natural healing approach, then show him or her this book and become a team.

Here's what you do, bearing in mind all the while that this represents an emergency situation:

As soon as your vet confirms that slough is imminent, make preparations for your horse's nutritional needs (Chapter 8) as well as his physical and emotional comfort. He probably won't be able to stand up for several days to a week following the slough; therefore, you will have to feed him and provide for his comfort during

American Farriers Journal

Corrosion by Pollit shows normal hoof (above, right) in contrast with hoof suffering from acute laminitis. Palpation of laminitic hoof will give familiar bounding pulse, characteristic of increased blood flow to rear portions of hoof. Flow is deficient to laminar attachments at face of P3 because nutrifying capillaries are now dysfunctional.

this period of forced recumbence.

For his physical comfort, he will require soft bedding to lay on. Large rubber stall mats will do, perhaps covered with hay — anything that will provide cushioning and can be cleaned of body wastes and temporary hoof secretions.

Assuming he has the will to live, then bring his horse buddy nearby, allowing them to nuzzle under your close supervision. Keep them close together from this point in time on.

Provide for his detoxification as well as per Chapter 9. It is my opinion that the strict adherence to the advice provided in these chapters is what ultimately is going to save your horse's life. With foreign chemicals removed from his system, flushed out by a natural diet, his traumatized hooves will take care of themselves with very little assistance from you.

Encourage him to eat and drink at all times he feels so inclined.

Now, the hooves:

Slough usually results from severe inflammation of the lamina and our failure to institute bona fide natural horse care that eliminates the cause of the laminitis. Even if your hoof care is reasonably natural, it will not prevent slough if the cause of the laminitis is not immediately arrested and supplanted with the necessary lifestyle changes.

It has been my observation that field vets will construe a presloughing hoof is suffering from infection, when in fact the inflamed laminar corium is over-secreting MMP-3/9 serum, as described earlier in this chapter. Hence, an oozing of yellow fluid may occur along the coronary corium, which is normal. Additionally, the entire foundered hoof will probably exude a characteristically obnoxious "founder smell," also normal, and which closely resembles thrush in its fetidness (— both conditions represent putrefaction of their respective epidermises). Consequently, vets will saturate the horse with antibiotics, or, in many instances, schedule emergency hoof wall resections — neither of which is indicated in the natural treatment of slough. They may have administered other medications for pain, blood treatment, and so forth.

Now refer to the photographs on page 31. This tragic case, involving a Quarter Horse over-drugged with antibiotics with no attention to changing his unnatural living conditions, sloughed all four hooves. In the lower photograph, taken immediately after the hooves detached, you can see that P3 has retreated somewhat into the folds of the skin surrounding the coronary corium. This is normal and to be expected. Leave it alone.

On closer examination, it may be seen that while much of P3, from its extensor process (top front of coffin bone) to the palmer processes (wings of coffin bone), is embedded in subcutaneous tissue, the lower crescent of the bone protrudes visibly. Instinctively, your horse will attempt to protect this part of his hoof by laying down and freeing the limb of weightbearing. During this stage, don't encourage the horse to move or stand up.

Within hours of slough, one of Nature's great miracles will unfold before your very eyes. Presuming that you have initiated the holistic changes called for, the surface of the coffin bone will begin to produce a spongy layer of protective horn.

What is happening is that the laminar epidermal cells adjoining the basal membrane will begin to proliferate a new inner hoof wall, called the *stratum lamellatum* (comprising the lamina we discussed earlier). It is divided into two interdigitated parts. The inner layer, called the primary epidermal lamellae, includes approximately 550-600 leaves which are produced in parallel rows along the surface of P3, perpendicular to the ground. Under normal conditions the long edges of the leaves facing away from P3 would attach to the fully keratinized hoof wall proper, called the *stratum medium*. Since the wall is gone, the lower reaches of the primary epidermal leaves will dry up and seal off the capillary network feeding them across the basal membrane. This action is tantamount to producing a protective band-aid. But it is only a temporary one, and I advise that you not cover P3 with a topical antiseptic or bandage wrap.

Simultaneously, further up the primary laminar epidermis, healing takes a different course. In close proximity to the coronary corium, where the hoof wall (tubular and intertubular horn) is produced around minute papillae, the primary lamellae begin immediately to produce keratinized horn at the neck of the hoof [recall Pollit: "Proliferating lamellar basal cells are confined to the proximal 10% of the lamellar inner hoof wall and are absent in the rest."]. This is accomplished by means of a secondary outer layer of specialized leaves, which are produced by the primary epidermal lamellae. According to Pollit:

> If the role of the epidermal lamellae is indeed suspensory, then an anatomical specialization increasing the surface area for the attachment of the multitude of caliginous fibers emanating from the outer surface of the distal phalanx [P3] would be expected. The secondary epidermal lamellae are just such a specialization. During the formation of an epidermal lamella, on the shoulders of the inner coronary groove, the basal cell layer proliferates causing folds (secondary lamellae) to form along the lamellar perimeter. The basal cell proliferation index is high on the shoulders of the coronary groove in the region of secondary lamella formation." [Pollit, EFJ (#84) 6/2000]

As laminar reconstruction takes place here at the neck of the hoof, a new wall will begin to emerge within weeks. Within six to nine months an entirely new wall will be re-grown. If the sole has detached, it, along with the heels, will reproduce almost completely within several weeks of slough. As soon as sufficient growth is in place, it is important to get the horse up and moving on his feet again. However, because of the loss of toe wall (which will take longer to reproduce), I advise strongly that as soon as the hoof is restored sufficiently to enable movement of the horse, fit him with hoof boots [see Resources]. From this point on, continue with the advice already presented for normally healing laminitic hooves.

White Line Disease

"White Line Disease," called WLD, and also known as "seedy toe," is a deterioration of the white line (junction between the outer wall and sole) wrought by a consortium of opportunistic and harmful bacteria and fungi. It is thought by some to be a consequence of dietary deficiency. Conceivably it arises from chronic laminitis, and for the same systemic reasons. Whatever, the infected hoof is trimmed no differently than the foundered one, and the same holistic measures brought to bear to arrest the laminitis, apply equally to destroying the pathogen base of this hoof infection.

To kill off the surface bacteria and fungi associated with WLD, your vet may recommend soaking the trimmed hoof for several days in a Clorox bath. But Chlorine is a powerful hydrophilic (water absorbing) agent and a known carcinogen — meaning, it will kill everything it comes in contact with and dry out the hoof. Therefore, I caution against its use. In severe cases, a vet may perform a wall resection (below). Avoid this procedure as well.

Alternatively, soak the infected hoof for five minutes in a mild solution of vinegar (i.e., 1 cup vinegar/3 gallons of water), twice a day for three days. This will create a pH environment within the infected area that is not conducive to the proliferation of the harmful microbes; nor will it dry out or harm newly regenerating laminar horn or healthy tissue still present. Between these vinegar soaks, apply sparingly liquid bee propolis that has been formulated for hooves (see Resources). Propolis, known for its powerful antibacterial, fungal, and viral properties, is produced naturally by bees to protect and sterilize their hives. It will not harm your horse's feet. Of course, such direct efforts to heal the hooves must always be carried out in the context of the broad, sweeping holistic lifestyle changes discussed in the following chapters.

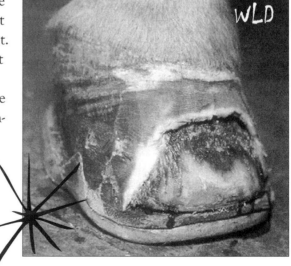

WLD

6 Freedom to move

Let them move, move, move! Horses that can't move freely are most prone to problems — neurotic habits, colic, stocked up legs, ligament aches and pains, and unhealthy hooves.
— Jaime Jackson (*Horse Owners Guide To Natural Hoof Care*)

Protagonists within the conventional veterinary and farriery community have in recent years argued against the viability of natural hoof care on the grounds that it is not possible within domestic horse stewardship. We are told in so many words, "Natural hooves are only possible among wild horses living in wild horse country. They do not apply to domesticated horses." They argue further that acutely laminitic horses need stall rest; in other words as little movement as possible during treatment and the early stages of rehabilitation. This position is justified, so they say, by the horse's obvious suffering.

Natural hoof care advocates are diametrically opposed to restricted movement or close confinement. And here is our reason:

> *Optimal circulation in the foundered hoof, essential for natural healing, is not possible without natural movement.*

Now, you're probably thinking, with some justification, "I don't really know what natural movement is, and regardless, my horse, who isn't wild, is too miserable to move even one step." Of course, from this perspective, most horse owners readily fall prey to the much advocated veterinary practice of close confinement. On the surface, it is all very logical.

Mustangs of Spirit Mountain

In the wild, horses frequent high elevation water holes to stand in and sooth their feet and bodies. Standing in water to heal is as natural to the horse as is drinking to quench his thirst. They are not stupid animals. They are survivors.

Instead, however, let's put your movement-relative-to-pain concerns into the context of our holistic perspective so you can take action to keep your horse out of that stall and get him going naturally just as soon as he is able to. Since the first mental blockade often concerns "natural movement," we'd better start there.

What is natural movement? Well, the good new is, you don't have to know what it is. All you need to do is provide the space for it to happen in, and your horse will take up his own natural movement as he sees fit. It's that simple. Horses instinctively know how to move naturally. You can't teach it to them, nor can you force it on them. They simply need adequate room to do it in. And a foundered horse needs the opportunity to move as naturally as he can and as much and as often as he can. Let me clarify.

Being no dummy, your horse will know which way to go, how far, and in what gait/speed to do it in. If you stall him, you've cut him off from doing anything but just standing there. Not unlike denying the horse his biomechanical need to assume the founder stance by trussing him up in bar shoes and foam sole supports, which keep him in a modified founder stance whether he needs it or not.

In the wild (our ideal holistic model for equine movement), horses move almost constantly, day and night. Nature designed them to do that. To keep moving. I know humans like to sit a lot, so the suggestion that constant movement 20 hours a day is a necessity can be hard to fathom. But horses aren't people. They sleep a few minutes or hours here and there, and stop to rest for a few minutes now and then. But that's all. They don't stand around doing nothing all day and all night long. Stall life isn't what nature intended. They are natural, semi-nomadic athletes, and what athlete can live a life of "bed rest" 20 hours a day, and then perform like an athlete for a few minutes that he is allowed to move?

But, you are thinking, 'My horse is in such great pain and I cannot stand the sight of his agony. I must do as the vet says, and put him back in his stall so that he does not harm himself by moving further on his tender feet and damaging them. For God's sake, his coffin bones are even pushing through his soles."

We natural hoof care practitioners view matters much differently, of course, or we wouldn't be advocating the seemingly "cruel." So, we would respond: "His founder was probably in part due to the *absence of sufficient natural movement*. So why heap more injustice on the original crime by depriving it altogether? Movement is synonymous with being a horse, moreover, he *requires* movement for a functioning hoof mechanism. And without the mechanism, healing is imperiled."

The idea, of course, is to strike a compromise between the horse's instinctual and biomechanical requirements to move naturally, in order to heal, and his limits imposed by the laminitic damage and pain. Even humans following surgery are encouraged to start moving (and relinquish pain medication therapy) as soon as possible, as it is known that this promotes healing. Every horse will respond differently, depending on his will to survive and the acuteness of his suffering. But, without the opportunity and incentive to move, he's at risk. What we recommend you do is this:

> Try to position your horse on relatively soft footing and encourage him to move forward gradually and incrementally.

Along the way, it's okay for the horse to lay down to "rest" his aching feet as much as he needs, even if he lays down longer than usual, even if all night. You might do the same under similar circumstances. But once he's up, it's time to move if he's able to. Even if he just stands there, that's a starting point. We want to establish a "starting point." Henceforth, we will measure our success, and set-backs (we'll probably run into a few), against this starting point. *Follow the horse's instincts to move.*

Some horse owners have sandy arenas, grassy fields, etc., to walk with their horses over. Obviously, you want to avoid gravelly or rocky surfaces, at least if such surfaces clearly bother him. In acute cases, I've advised some horse owners to lay out a path of rubber mats (e.g., stall mats, horse trailer mats) for the horse to walk on. Leading him down the center aisle of a barn will work (not a bad idea if it's the middle of winter and the ground is icy and craggy). What's important is that we provide the horse with an acceptable space to move across.

In the worst cases, it'll be tough going at first. Reward the horse at every step. Set a schedule with a series of goals and rewards. For example, if the horse can only take one or two steps. Bravo! Let him know that you appreciate his efforts. Dote over him and/or give him a small treat (chopped carrot, apple, etc. – and, yes, it's okay to feed a laminitic horse). Then release him from his halter and let him do his own thing. Maybe he won't move at all, maybe he'll lay down again, maybe he'll move a little more. Just accept whatever it is. An hour later, and not a minute more, return and try it again. If he needs more "rest" time, let him rest, and wait another hour, or two, or three, or whatever he thinks he needs. Just because he's down doesn't mean you're going to have to "put him down." Otherwise, encourage him to move on the hour (or whatever the acceptable time interval is to him). And dote over and reward him again and again for every gallant effort he makes.

If he has a horse pal, as I've mentioned, keep him close at hand, especially now as we begin to encourage movement. There is no better stimulus than a buddy to get a horse going. Keep them both together at liberty, if they are compatible, so they can nuzzle and mutually groom each other. They are social animals and *require* constant companionship. Now think about this:

> *Horses require physical contact to be emotionally and psychologically healthy. A psychologically healthy horse will heal easier than one who is not.*

In the past, before I became a natural hoof care provider, I can recall foundered horses that died in their pain from stress and isolation. They just gave up. This is something to be concerned about. Having a horse buddy around, and doting over your horse, lets him know you really care. He'll try harder, and he will be less likely to give up. And die.

Gradually increase the duration of the walking sessions while he's under halter. Don't use a whip to force him to move. *Ask him to move*, and give him time to respond. He'll move when he's ready and able to. Gauge his progress hour to hour, then day to day, and then week to week, and so forth. Keep a chart to record his progress. It has been my observation that many foundered horses are sent off to slaughter because their owners didn't know how to gauge progress.

Depending on the cause and severity of his laminitis, he may "sound out" of the attack very quickly and literally become rideable in a day or two; or he may take longer, months. Horses that aren't making good progress within 3 or 4 months probably aren't being treated as effectively as they could be, but let's be lenient. Go with the flow. But make sure you aren't paddling upstream against the healing current. Know where you're heading and learn to gauge his progress. Your chart will give clues about his rate of healing. Now, think about this:

> We want as our goal for your horse to be sound and rideable in hoof boots no more than 6 months after you've begun this program. No matter how bad his founder is at present.

The very worst cases, with hoof slough, may require up to nine months (although a sufficiently regenerated hoof for natural move- ment is possible in as little as six weeks). But most cases should be cleared up with several weeks to several months. If your horse's feet continue to re-founder, than at issue are other changes in the horse's life that need closer scrutiny. We're going to discuss and disarm those right now, so relax.

7 Creating a founder free habitat

In addition to providing the welcome soft mud, sand, and moisture around the watering hole, the horse owner should make sure that the remainder of the pasture is dry and that the ground is firm, even rocky in places. — Jaime Jackson (*The Natural Horse*, 1992)

Pastures, green pastures that is, are not natural to the horse. They are time bombs waiting to go off: the greener, the lusher, the deadlier.
— Jaime Jackson (4-H Clinic, Little Rock Arkansas, 1993)

Ideally, we want to provide your foundered horse with a pasture to live in. The right kind of pasture is important, however. Not just any pasture will do. If it's not the right kind of pasture, he will probably be better off living in a paddock. Which is okay, and will work, although a paddock is less desirable than the right kind of pasture, if it's available. Either way, if we can get his living space right, most of our founder problems will be over with once and for all.

The ideal horse pasture resembles wild horse country, which is a high desert type environment. If you live with your horses somewhere in the U.S. Great Basin, then you know what I'm talking about. I've described wild horse country in my book, *The Natural Horse* (see Resources), and will refer you to that text to learn more about the subject if it is new to you.

Wild horse country closely resembles the ancient homeland of the modern horse: North Africa, Mesopotamia, and other arid, high desert enclaves of middle Asia. And many of our wild horses are direct descendents of horses that came from those far off, exotic sounding places. I don't think we should ignore this connection because, from an evolutionary standpoint, our horses today aren't that far removed from this ancestral and biological matrix. Indeed, bananas grow naturally best in certain environments, and so do horses.

Think about it: It wasn't that long ago that Spanish Conquistadors introduced Arabian-influenced bloodlines into the New World. The Castilians, like the ancient Romans before them, much coveted the sturdy desert steeds of the Moors, Bedouins, Turks, and others, for their riding and breeding stock. The Spanish crossed these bloodlines with larger, European horses. The new Spanish breeds, the Andalusians, along with the pure blood Arabian lines, have heavily influenced the current breeds we know today, including, significantly, their digestive peculiarities.

It's no wonder that wild horses, and wild asses (the earliest burro herds were derived from Spanish remudas), have proliferated so successfully in the U.S. Great Basin. In a sense, they've entered a surrogate womb, a high desert biome niche, which fulfills their ancient habitat requirements. One astute old timer I talked with years ago in Nevada was right, in a sense, when he said, "Heck, mustangs grow like weeds out here."

But most horse owners cannot put their foundered horses in wild horse country to heal. For them, such land is neither available nor practical to get to. Fortunately, it isn't necessary to do so, either. Nor would I recommend it.

That's because we can simulate habitat conditions characteristic of wild horse country right in our own backyards. We must learn to convert our horses' living spaces into natural habitats based on the wild horse country model. And for our foundered horses, we need to do this as quick as possible.

Practically speaking, how do we do this?

Work with the space you've got

First, with one exception, work with the space you've got. If your horse is stabled in a stall, then plan to make arrangements to get him out of it as soon as possible. Stalls preclude constant movement and normal socialization; as such, they constitute founder traps. His new home should be either a paddock or a pasture.

Dry pasture or no pasture at all

The only suitable, natural pasture for a horse is of the high desert type — barren and sprinkled lightly with bunch grasses, sparse forage, and an abundance of rocks. If your current pasture is full of green grasses and legumes, then it probably isn't the right type (for reasons that I'll explain in the next chapter). Either disc plow his field until the turf is killed off, or get him out and put him into a smaller disked field or dirt paddock. In other words, "dry lot"

him. It is extremely risky to return a foundered horse to a grass pasture, even if the green grass is "burnt up" in summer, or has died down to stub and is dormant in winter, because founder causing agents can quickly surface in the grasses and legumes if rapid growth occurs (e.g., following a rain or sudden rise in temperature).

Space to move in

The living space should be big enough for at least two to three compatible horses to move around in comfortably together. An acre is more than enough space. Of course, if you have hundreds of acres of high desert type habitat to put your horse into, all the better. The more space available, the less you'll have to exercise him.

How much exercise will your foundered horse need? As I explained in the previous chapter, he'll need much less movement

Rocky Mountain high desert pasture

than what is considered normal and natural during his early heal-ing phase (first three to six months). Later, after healing, he'll re-quire 10 to 15 miles per day of movement for optimal health and a founder-free life. This can be achieved in various ways, including going for rides together, lunging, socialization (playing with his horse buddies), and creative feeding practices.

During 1999, I traveled to Europe to observe several natural boarding arrangements that were scaled down to paddock size. One paddock was several hundred feet long, and 50 feet or so wide. Filled with trees, large rocks and boulders, various shrubs, it was impossible to see from one end to the other. Three horses roamed in it together and seemed happy as can be. A path with intermittently placed miniature hay racks were stocked 24 hours a day with different grass hays. Others "treats" were added to the racks during the day. A "swamp" surrounded the watering trough for soaking the hooves. Rubber bricks were mortised together to form walking trails throughout the paddock, so that the horses would not have to walk in constant mud during winter. Twice a week the horses (all barefooted and in their twenties or thirties) were removed for extended rides in the nearby mountains. My opinion is that this paddock arrangement, carved out of a small corner of a ten acre tract of land, was virtually founder proof.

Diverse footing

Ideally, the soil and terrain of your horse's living space will vary considerably: sand, dirt, gumbo, rock . . . flat, hilly, mountainous. This diversity aids in challenging, and wearing, the hooves more naturally. But if all you have is flat dirt, that'll work too. It will simply mean that you'll have to provide more natural trims to com-pensate for the lack of natural wear.

Ironically, some horse owners will go to great lengths to alter their horses' habitats, making them less natural while thinking they've made improvements. Several years ago, I was called to a large ranch where three mares had foundered within weeks of each other (all were eventually euthanized). The distraught owner had been deluged with a range of conflicting explanations for their laminitic attacks by a stream of veterinary and farriery practitioners she had consulted with. By the time I was called in for an opinion, the owner had spent a fortune disc-plowing her fescue pastures (having been led to believe they were the leading suspect in the founder outbreak, which was partly true in her case) and even hired a team of workers to hand pick thousands of rocks from them (which one of the vets said may have been what caused the founder). A towering "mountain" of rocks, over twenty feet high and fifty feet across at the base, had been created! I couldn't believe my eyes. Of course, right off the bat I lost all my credibility with the owner, and her staff, when my first piece of advice was to return every last rock to the fields from whence they came!

In case you are wondering, wild horse country can get pretty rocky, and the horses are capable of galloping over it without harming their feet. But most of the time the bands step between rocks on the alluvial fans, sandy creek bottoms, and elsewhere. While not rock hard, such ground is extremely abrasive and contributes to the natural wear of their hooves. These diverse footings do much to hone their picture perfect hooves, and at the same time cause them to exercise their bodies, generating, as stated above, an army of slender, muscular, and "powerful" equine athletes.

Now, come winter, wild horse country can get pretty muddy between all those rocks. And I've tracked bands sloshing through knee-deep gumbo for miles. Often, they'll keep to the rocks to prevent sinking into the muck. So, if you have concerns about winter mud harming your horse's feet, don't worry — Nature designed those hooves to adapt.

Speaking of rocks, it is a fact that many horse owners, and hoof care professionals, gauge the viability of natural hoof care and bare-footedness on the ability of horses to move pain free over rocks, gravel, pavement, and other hard surfaces. I always advise using quality hoof boots when riding over such ground, however, reminding clients and others that the purpose of natural hoof care is to give their horses the opportunity to go barefooted when not being ridden so that their feet can become healthier from natural wear. Horses, including your foundered horse, under no circumstances should be forced to move or live exclusively upon rocks, as that would not be natural. Our wild horses prove only that movement over rock *some of the time* is not harmful to their feet.

> *Properly trimmed and conditioned barefooted horses should be rideable a minimum of 3 to 5 miles at a time over gravel or paved roads without problems. The same horses should be rideable barefooted over varied, but rugged terrain from 15 to 100 miles per ride. If you are using properly fitted Swiss Horse Boots, and the horse is properly conditioned, then virtually all hoof related hypersensitivity issues are eliminated. Use boots always if you are concerned or uncertain.*

But assuming that your horse's habitat is relatively flat and composed principally of packed dirt, sand, or loam, then you will have to compensate for the lack of abrasion by providing your horse with more frequent natural trims (approximately every 3 to 4 weeks). Bracy Clark, a famous English veterinary researcher showed two hundred years ago that regularly exercised and naturally trimmed horses living in paddocks could sustain healthy, uncontracted feet. Back in the 1980's, I personally trimmed several hundred Peruvian Pasos over a three and a half year period, and can testify that they all had healthy, lameness-free, naturally shaped hooves. With one exception, all of these horses — stallions, mares, and their offspring — lived in small paddocks, but were afforded regular daily pasture turnout and exercise sessions with their trainers and handlers. The one horse with problem feet had been foundered several years earlier, and remained foundered the entire time I cared for him. He was, however, the only horse on the premises that was shod (by me, as it turns out). This was many years ago, because I didn't know then what I'm telling you about now.

Moisture for the hooves

A natural pasture will also have a water hole, pond, stream, or some body of water that your horse can step into while he drinks. Water conditions and cleans the hooves. It's not only good for the hooves, it's *necessary* for optimal hoof function. The mechanism functions at its best if the hooves are "lubed" with water and mud daily. In the wild, horses stand in the water long enough to drink and, depending on the weather and time of year, bathe. Five, 10, 15 minutes of watering behavior per day is good for your horse's feet. Now, if you don't have a watering hole, make one! Let your water trough overflow and render a muddy area. Or make a 4 x 8 foot, 6 inch deep recession in the ground and line it with heavy plastic sheeting (e.g., visqueen) or cement, covered with sand (sand is just as good as mud) — or cover the plastic with rubber bricks, or a rubber stall mat — and watered down to make a slurry. Some horse owners I know use "foot baths" used by sheep and cattle ranchers to treat hoof infections.

I have been asked numerous times: Is it a good idea to soak foundered hooves in water or mud? Yes. If your horse is foundered, lead him to the watering hole and let him decide if he wants to stand in it and for how long. He'll know what's best for him. Which brings to mind another story . . .

I remember years ago a horse that was foundered in a barn where I normally did not work. No one was there this particular day but me, and I happened to walk by the horse's tiny paddock (actually a stall without a roof). Well there he was perched on "all fours" in the founder stance in an old Eagle-Claw bathtub which the owners had filled with water. To this day, I don't know for certain if the water was intended for him to drink from, or soothe his aching feet! He also had one of those tiny stall waterers mounted on the fence next to the tub. And since it worked, I can only conclude the tub was there for the purpose of founder relief.

Snow doesn't bother the horse's feet either, and the wild ones seem to enjoy romping in it. They also eat snow for water as much as they paw through it to get at vegetation. If snow is available, lead your horse onto it, and if it brings him temporary relief, leave him there until he's ready to leave of his own accord. According to

Pollit:

> Trials to determine the effects of a slurry of iced water applied to the feet of [domestic] horses are underway. Preliminary results show that horses, unlike humans, do not regard extremely cold feet as uncomfortable and can tolerate having their feet in iced water for 48 hours with no ill effect.[†]

Pasture as a food supply

I can remember as clear as the setting sun the first thing that came to mind when I spent my first day among the wild ones. "There's nothing to eat here." It was not until I looked at the total picture, "distance x nibbling," that I began to grasp just how plentiful the nutritional landscape actually was.

In no way can I advise readers here on what constitutes the precise natural diet of a wild horse. They eat so many different things, the names of which I don't even know, and things I didn't really pay attention to, that I could only mislead the uninformed. I'm neither a botanist nor a nutritionist. In my defense, however, as early as the 1980's I was calling upon the equine research community to investigate the flora constituting the wild horse diet. To my knowledge, no one yet has undertaken this badly needed research.

On the other hand, I'm prepared to say that most of their bulk diet is composed of dry bunch-type grasses, hence, the sobriquet, "hay burner," is very be-fitting the horse. A munch here, and a munch there, 20 hours a day of munching dry grasses is the natural order of their day. In betwixt, there's also a constant nibbling of stems, bark, and leaves of hundreds of different kinds of plants, cacti, trees, berries, and nuts which seem to deliver needed micronutrients. A University of Nevada master's thesis on wild horse "dung" content done thirty years ago testifies to the large variety of vegetation horses' naturally consume.[‡]

[†]C. Pollit, "Equine Laminitis: A Revised Pathophysiology," European Farriers Journal, #85, 8/2000.

[‡]See Zarn, Heller, Collins. "Wild Free-Roaming Horses — Present Knowledge" Technical Note 294. USDOI and USFS, March, 1977.

On film, I have an interesting example of how wild horses apparently extract some of their mineral needs from their environment. A family band, wielding their hooves like pick-axes, literally hacks away at the ground near a dry stream bed, prying loose chunks of white rock. All together, a dozen members strong, the wild ones grind and masticate this calcareous rock into a chalky cloud that nearly hides the horses! This grinding not only meets nutritional needs, it obviously wears and polishes their molars. (Could this be nature's version of "floating the teeth" sans a vet?)

The natural pasture provides other, less obvious, nutrients needed by horses. Ironically, these are derived from the horses themselves in the form of dung beds. Commonly a trait among the very young, dung eating must be included as part of the natural feedscape of wild horse county. Maybe it has to do with digestion. Maybe it has to do with developing resistance to parasites — including those apparently responsible for founder. I only know that, however despicable it may seem to our species, it is somehow natural and therefore necessary to theirs. So, it is my opinion that the practice of cleaning paddocks and pastures of dung, ostensibly to prevent the spread of disease and parasites, ought — in view of the potential harm of chemical parasiticides to the horse's digestive system — to be re-evaluated by veterinary researchers.

Until that day, however, I recommend that your founder-free habitat be kept reasonably clean of dung, or that the dung at least be kept to one area of the paddock. For example, in the wild, bands of mustangs will regularly visit "stud piles" to defecate upon. Apparently, these are markers to let other bands in the area know of their mutual presence. As with dung eating behavior (coprophagy), the creation and sustaining of these dung piles does not appear to bring harm to the horses.

Avoiding "founder traps"

It is my opinion that "green pastures" are not the natural habitat of the horse. Cattle, maybe, horses not. Nowhere in wild horse country do horses walk upon the food they eat. There are no vast carpets of thick, green grass. They just aren't there. And, if they were there, it's just possible there might not be any wild horse herds left. At least not completely sound ones.

Thinking back to the prologue of this book, the riparian nightmare that took place in the Warners was a fluke. The horses were trapped by human fences in an area closed off to natural defoliation, not unlike a "sugar freak" trapped inside a candy store. My visits to wild horse country since reveal the opposite — normally, wild horses visit riparians (unfenced) only long enough to drink and engage in other normal watering behavior.[†] Then they leave. The lush grasses, where present, don't hold that much interest for them, for whatever reason, including inter-band competition (driven by stallion rivalry) or justifiable fear of predators — mountain lions attack foals in the wild. Lingering indefinitely at a lush riparian carries risks for the mustang, and they know it.

Legume fields, and even legume hays, are, in my opinion, time bombs. They are prescriptions for founder. Most of the laminitic horses I'm dealing with nationwide have been fed legumes of one type or another. As soon as the legumes are removed permanently from their horses' diets, laminitic inflammation invariably begins to recede.

Legumes [Latin: *plants with seed pods*] are plants classified as members of the "pea" family, and from them are derived the "hot" hays that we are all familiar with: alfalfa, clover, vetch, and lespedeza (named after an 18th-century Spanish governor of Florida), among others. It may be that some horses, more than others, are sensitive to legumes, and thus are prone to founder from it. Perhaps it has something to do with the type of bacteria that reside in the nodules of the legume roots, and which fix the nitrogen that the plant needs for food. Maybe there's something in the plant "flowers" which upset the digestive enzymes in the horse's cecum, which then give rise

---

[†]Confirmed also by Karen Sussman, President of the International Society for the Preservation of Mustangs and Burros (ISPMB), who agrees that riparians are not the magnets for wild horses that anti-mustang advocates claim (— generally ranchers who argue the horses compete for scarce water with domestic cattle on leased BLM land).

to toxins that proliferate and enter the horse's blood system. Whatever the causal or catalytic relationship, I've got red flags up on leguminous plants, and their hays. I'd advise you to be on guard if your horse has foundered and these plants are in your horse's feed program. Horse and legumes must be separated.

But not all grasses can be considered safe, either. Fescue grass has a near notorious relationship to founder, giving title to the notorious "fescue foot," a term that should, in the minds of readers, be synonymous with a "stretched white line," one of the hallmarks of founder. Across the Southern U.S, fescue probably precipitates more bouts of laminitis than any other single cause (with the possible exception of over-graining). Other grasses consumed green are probably also dangerous; recent research suggests that all temperate grasses may accumulate specific sugars (e.g., fructans) during cold snaps that are then consumed in harmful concentrations by the horse, resulting in founder.[†]

That the incidence of founder abates during the mid-summer and winter months, when otherwise green pastures are either dried up or dormant, is a sign that the perpetual "dry" bunch grasses of wild horse country, tantamount to domestic grass hay, is a direction our feeding programs need to go in. I practically despair now when I see horses turned out onto green fields, knee deep, at any time of the year, no matter what kind of grass or legume. And there's no telling how many horses succumb to slaughter as a consequence of these grassy "founder traps" nationwide each year.

My advice? Remove your horse, laminitic or not, from any green pasture, or at least during their rapid growth phases or at any time they are lush. Be wary of mowing or bush-hogging and thinking you are "safe" — new, green, lush grasses are often pushing up thru the stubble, especially after a rain or temperature change. Better yet, move him permanently into a dry lot paddock. If you pasture your horse in a high desert type biome — wild horse country, in other words — then keep him there, providing he's not mired in a riparian.

[†]Reilly, J.D., 1998 International Research Conference on Equine Laminitis

7 Diet per se

An unexpected research finding that may have great practical
significance is that experimental animals live longer with much lower
rates of disease when they consume less than the recommended daily
allowance of calories. – Andrew Weil, M.D. (*Spontaneous Healing*)

Founder is intrinsically complex. All things equal, not all
horses demonstrate the same resistance or proneness to becoming
laminitic. Two horses being fed the same things may never founder, or both may founder, or either one may founder while the
other remains founder free. However, I believe the propensity for
foundering is almost certainly there in all horses. Only the degree
to which each horse is vulnerable varies, just like humans vary
widely in their individual genetic tolerances to diseases.

Whatever individual tolerances to laminitis may exist, diet
seems to lie at the center of its causality. My experience has been
this: the more unnatural the horse's diet and eating behavior, the
greater his risk of becoming laminitic. Now, we can ignore this
and turn laminitis into some kind of crap shoot – in other words,
keep feeding your horse the same way and hope that his diet is
okay and that he is in someway one of the lucky, founder-resistant
ones. Or, we can heed the natural dietary prerogatives and do
something about it. With thousands of horses foundering every
year, the stakes are high if you decide to take a wait and see attitude.

Some horses, especially the overfed fat ones with "cresty" necks,
have long been targeted as prime founder candidates. But any
horse, regardless of body type or degree of being overweight, can
founder, so our dietary approach must encompass unnatural eating

habits, regardless of a horse's weight. I believe that our wild horses, and wild horse country itself, provide vital clues concerning the actual meaning of natural diet — feed, and feeding behavior.

So, much of this chapter is aimed at connecting the laminitic horse to his primitive, but successful, dietary roots based on the wild horse, and wild horse country, model. It's really very simple. And it works. With it, I'll take any fat, founder-footed caricature of a horse, regardless of his body type, and turn him into a lean, fit fellow with sound, founder-free hooves and an eagerness to run and frolic.

Meal time: starving our horses into fatness

In the wild, horses spend much of their daily lives nibbling at this and that. They slowly move along, hour after hour, 20 hours a day, heads down for the most part, nibbling. Ravenous "pig outs" are not possible. There are no sudden buckets of grain, free-choice vitamin concentrates, or rich green grasses there on the

ground waiting for them to gorge themselves on. To get what they need, they must work for it — via natural movement — and even then they will only get it in small quantities at a time.

This is no freak accident. Nature intended it this way, although you couldn't convince me in view of how we do things back "over here" in the domestic horse world. The horse's body has been designed by nature to consume food in relatively small quantities, spread out over many hours per day, day and night.

BLM fence line divides typical sparse habitat of wild horse country from atypical domestic-like pasture created in government riparian study.

Appreciate this fact, and you are one giant step closer to understanding why so many horses founder.

Now, let's think about how most domestic horses are probably fed. Typically, they are fed like humans, in "set" meals, normally once, twice, and very occasionally three times per day (if the owner's schedule permits). Enough hay is given that they can "finish off" in a meal — for "waste not, want not." Along with these "spaced" hay rations, they are often given "vitamin" concentrates (whether they need them or not); grain, such as oats, sweet feed, or some kind of pelleted grain/vitamin/hay formulation; biotin supplements for the hooves; and many other things. To liven up the horse's taste buds, or to sneak in any oral medications the horse happens to be on (e.g., thyroid supplements), grains may be laced with corn oil and molasses or some other kind of sweetener.

On top of all of the above, the horse's diet can be altered dramatically at any moment, depending on the vicissitudes of the hay market, the fashions and availability of high tech grains/grain-formulations of the moment, pasture availability, and the owner's pocketbook and busy schedule. Which is to say that inconsistency and convenience often command domestic horse diets.

Now, what's wrong with this picture? Plenty!

Foremost, and this may come as a surprise, we are starving our horses by feeding them everything they can finish off in a meal. That's right, and the "psychology" behind their starvation predicament is no different than humans laboring under a starvation-type diet. Let's think about this, for a moment.

If you are hungry, and someone says to you that you cannot eat until the arrival of some arbitrary set time, what is the message your body is getting? Hunger. Now, let's really extend the period of abstinence, and, while we're at it, reduce your food allotment. How is your body going to respond to this deprivation? Starvation.

So, when the moment finally arrives that you can no longer stand the deprivation, and you "give in," what are you going to do? Pig out. And every nutritionist on the face of the earth will tell you that when you crash diet and pig out on a regular basis, you're actually throwing your body into metabolic disorder. Biologically, to stave off starvation, your body is genetically equipped to resist loss of body mass (i.e., fat) while increasing carbohydrate (sugars) uptake to add more mass to offset the next starvation cycle. So, typically, you'll probably end up heavier than when you started the diet. In other words, you are going to get fatter.

The very plight of most domestic horses.

Now, we might elect instead to revel at the sight of plump horses running around us, and how happy they must be all fatted up! But the truth is, these "fat" horses are actually starving. They are overweight because they have been conditioned by us to over-eat in order to survive. Again, just like a person bingeing on a starvation diet. We are giving them more than they should eat at once, but less than what they need per day. What is the horse to do?

Let's say they "follow their instincts," and *dare* to eat less than we have offered them. Maybe even leave some of that hay on the ground because, instinctively, something inside them says don't eat it all at once, "or else." Should a horse do this, of course, they run the risk of their rations being cut back. For, once more, "waste not, want not," and I have not met a horse owner in 25 years who has not threatened to cut back a feed ration where the horse has not finished his plate repeatedly.

Perhaps a fat horse wouldn't matter if it weren't the case that he is also a founder victim (or candidate) for it. Indeed, what horse owner today isn't chided by the vet or horsey magazine, that her overweight equine companion is at risk of founder? So, what do you do about it? That's right, more starvation. Which, we know from the dietary nutritionists, only fuels the fires of weight reten-tion. A starving body will do everything it can to stave off weight loss. It has to if the body is to survive.

Most horse owners with foundered horses who consult profes-sionally with me have run right into this wall. "My horse is over-weight and I can't get him to lose it." Most fear, rightfully so as it turns out, that if they withhold their feed to any further extent, their horses may just keel over and die. Which happens. The problem is often further exacerbated if other horses are compounded with the foundered one and there is competition for "available forage." How can you reduce the ration of one, without starving the others? Thus, it is common that many foundered horses I'm confronted with are overweight and there is seemingly nothing the horse owner can do about it, save, literally, to starve the horse, and his companions, to death.

We don't want to do that.

The nature of natural equine digestion

Before I advise you what to do, let's return to the discussion of the horse's digestive system. We need to jump start our holistic nutrition program in a new direction to deal with the fatness issue, but we need a little more information before acting. To help, I'd like to refer to Eva Muller, a Certified Hoof Care Specialist from Switzerland, who also holds an agricultural degree in the animal sciences:

> Horses are single-stomached herbivores which are capable of digesting large amounts of fiber in their diet, largely through a process of microbial fermentation within the digestive tract. Approximately 60 percent of the digestion consists of this microbial fermentation which takes place in the caecum and large intestine. Thus, when feeding a horse, we must think of feeding the microbes properly: sufficient roughage and proteins, no sudden change of food! [*Hoof Care Advisor*, Sept/Oct 1999]

What Eva is referring to here are the digestive "bugs" living in the horse's stomach and gut. They, not just the horse, have to be fed properly too. Or they get upset and enable the proliferation of harmful bacteria living among them in there. To prevent this from happening, these "microbes" must be fed all the time and in small quantities — just like we see happening in wild horse country. Neither the horse nor the microbes living within him synergistically appreciate this starvation business.

The dilemma, of course, is how to satisfy the appetites of both critters at the same time. The horse, overweight, one would think needs less food; but dare to oblige that and we risk aggravating the equally hungry digestive microbes. What do you do?

Well, this may sound crazy, but to save your foundered horse, you must now feed him all the roughage he can stand to eat. Pile it on, and keep piling it on, until he walks away from it, as though if he eats another bite, he might explode! If there are other horses "starving" in his paddock or pasture with him, pile it in front of them too. Dare them all to explode together! But be sure you are feeding him the proper things!

What is at work here is our effort to break the psychology of the "starvation" syndrome your horse is caught up in. We want your horse to free himself from his starvation diet by doing what comes natural to him: eating only when he is hungry (which is much of the time, all day and all night long), and in the smaller quantities his digestive system can best tolerate (which also satisfies the microbes).

I know this advice may seem frightful to some readers, but really, it's nature's way for your horse. Especially foundered horses. And they will transition metabolically to lean bodies with healthy digestive tracts if you give them time. Be patient and allow at least six months for the weight reduction to become noticeable.

Does the same advice apply to "skinny" horses? It applies equally to all horse types — ectomorphic, endomorphic, mesomorphic. Underweight horses will gain weight, overweight horses will lose weight, and so forth.

Meanwhile, your horse must be encouraged to move, as I've already explained. Although "exercise" is a dreaded word for overweight human couch potatoes guilty of crash dieting, your horse will welcome the opportunity to move 20 hours a day, because that's what nature designed him to do. Horses are not sedentary creatures, but require almost constant movement in a nibbling posture for healthy digestion. Natural movement, in addition to healing the hooves, also burns calories.

Fortunately, the calories in hay are easy to "burn off". And since hay is going to be the principal foodstuff for your horse from this day forward, it won't take long for him to start slimming down. Perhaps you can find some additional comfort in the wise words of Dr. James Rooney:

> It is certainly true that we know all too little about the nutritional needs of the horse. Many authorities tell us so. I do not accept the corollary that we do not know how to feed horses. [While] I hasten to say that I support intensive, careful research on nutrition of horses . . . when the work is done, however, I venture to predict that grass, timothy hay, and oats will stand untarnished in the scientific array. The horse evolved and developed a digestive system specifically adapted to roughage as the primary food source. The natural horse spends much of his time grazing or munching dry grass — hay. [The Lame Horse]

I'll address the horse's protein needs shortly.

Hay schedule

I suspect that Professor Pollit's laminitis research is on the money: there are enzymatic imbalances raging out of control in the foundered hoof, stimulated by harmful bacteria in the horse's digestive system. But by providing unlimited dry grass (non-legume) hays, you can set your horse in one fell swoop on an entirely new holistic course of healing. And this brings us to one of the fundamental principles of feeding in our natural horse care movement:

> All horses should be provided with a range of free-choice (non-legume or fescue) grass hays, 24 hours a day.

Paradoxically, then, it is necessary to feed "more" to "lose" weight. If an unlimited supply of dry grass (tantamount to hay) were a real concern, then every free-roaming wild horse in the world would be foundered. Which is not the case.

Kinds of hay to feed

Plan ahead and purchase more than one type of grass hay. Buy several bales of each and keep them around. Test your horse to see which he prefers, and when he prefers to eat them. See if his preferences change over a period of time. Chances are good that they will. In the wild, horses adapt to eating things in season. Albeit these dietary changes are gradual, but they do represent adaptive responses and the need to eat different things.

What kind of hays should we put out? I've already warned against using legumes (Alfalfa, Clovers, vetch, lespedeza, etc. — see overleaf, page 114) and fescues, at least until convincing research shows how to feed them safely, or determines that some horses are indeed more founder-prone than others when fed them, or alters them genetically to render them safe. This leaves the grass hays, with the exception of fescue, which appears dangerous during its rapid growth phases (fall and spring), or any time it is lush and green. See what's available in your area, or what hay brokers can import into your area. Hays I've had success with are oat, orchard, brome, Timothy (see overleaf, page 115). Many others exist — do some research; you might also take a look at what's in your pasture and try to identify what's in it. As I mentioned earlier, what a blessing it would be if equine nutritionists would study the grass forages in wild horse country. Unquestionably, those grasses (and other forage) could be cultivated in domestication, harvested, and sold to horse owners in various forms as natural forage and "founder guards."

How to feed hay

Feed the hay on the ground, or, as I observed being done in the paddocks mentioned earlier in Europe, build mini hay mangers that stand on the ground. Place them along a path from one end of a very long paddock to the other. Horses will instinctively travel

(overleaf) legumes and grasses)

Legumes

Avoid feeding your foundered horse any of these legumes or their near relatives.

Alfalfa is identified by the "sawtooth" tip of the leaflet. The bloom of alfalfa has multiple flowers. Color may vary from white to purple.

Red clover and white clover are true clovers. As with all true clovers, the three leaflets are attached to the stem at the same point. The most widely planted clover is red clover, mostly because it is easy to establish. Red clover stems and leaves are hairy. There is often a pale green, V-shaped mark on the top side of the leaf. The flowers form a small, reddish colored ball.

Birdsfoot trefoil is a common pasture legume. It does well alone or mixed with cool season grasses. It is easily identified by the five leaflets per leaf The bright yellow blooms can also aid in Identification.

Crownvetch is another forage. One of its prime uses is on road banks. Its dense foliage has made it useful for erosion control. It is easily identified by the leaves. There are seven-fifteen pairs of leaflets per leaf. The flowers are pea-like and range in color from white to purple.

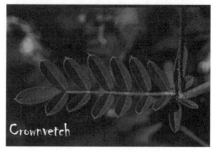

Try using these grasses in hay form only
to feed your foundered horse.

Grasses

Bromegrass is an excellent,
sod-forming forage producer.

Orchardgrass is fairly shade tolerant. It's a tall bunch grass. In immature stages, there
is a papery membrane where the leaf attaches to the main stem. This often tears into
shreds as plant heads out. The young stems are flat, and the leaves are V-shaped.

Timothy, mainly a hay crop, has leaves
rolled in the bud shoot and the membrane is
notched on one or both sides. Its easily recognizable
head is densely flowered, cylindrical and spike-like.

from one to the next all day long, nibbling different hays as they go. "Eat and go" is the natural order of all horses.

The reason we don't want to feed hay much further off the ground than the mini-mangers has to do with the horse's natural respiration and digestion — explanations for which, once more, must be sought at the doors of natural selection. Why do horses naturally graze in the wild with their heads down? While they do this instinctively and unconsciously, we are challenged to think why they do it this way so as not to force them to do it otherwise for our own convenience and, in so doing, create problems for them. Such as dust particles that are more apt to irritate the mucous membranes of the respiratory tract when the bend of the neck is forced by compelling the animal to eat at the "table height" levels of typical hay mangers. Respiratory infections and diseases may result. Which we are strained to find anywhere in wild horse country. Certainly this is cause for reflection when we observe "difficult" domestic horses which are determine to pull their hay from their mangers in order to eat it off the ground. Is there a message here?

Grain

Feeding grain concentrates may be very good for the pocketbooks of the "grain industry," but they can also be additional founder traps for the horse. Of course, horses "love" grain and horse owners "love" to feed it to them. It's kind of a "co-dependent" relationship. The horse is probably starving (for the reasons given above) and horse owners don't want their horses to starve. Add the profit incentive to rich, sweetened grain concentrates with all sorts of scientific claims purporting them to be in the best interest of your horse, and you have another prescription for founder.

The addition of grain to the horse's diet should be based on genuine protein requirements. Those of us in the natural horse care movement believe that plain whole or crimped oats are probably the best and safest of the grains to feed horses. A handful of "sweet feed" thrown in won't hurt the horse, and will add some nutrition, and possibly make his meal more palatable. We do advocate against wheat grains (e.g., chops), and also do not recommend barley; Xenophon's contemporaries wrote 2500 years ago of problems associated with "barley foot" — which was surely founder — among horses of Ancient Greece.

How much grain? You'll have to experiment through observation and experimentation. Working horses and lactating mares are thought by some equine nutritionists to need more than idle horses. However, our aim is not to create idle horses or induce carbohydrate overload in working horses. In the wild, all horses "work", and lactating mares eat the same vegetation that other band members access. And nowhere in wild horse country are there "buckets of grain" sitting there for binges. Hence, I advise horse owners to be very cautious and to dole out grains piecemeal, in smaller amounts with greater frequency. This is especially true for your foundered horse, whose digestive system was probably already overloaded.

So, a small coffee can of oats per day is probably more than enough for most average sized horses. Half in the morning, the rest at the end of the day. Or spread it out in three meals. If you're using a mini-manger with a rounded bottom constructed like a feed trough, break the hay apart and sprinkle the grain into the hay. It only takes a minute. I've done this, and your horse will eat the oats right along with the hay. Kind of an "equine granola."

I recommend that you follow this graining program even if your horse just foundered yesterday from "carbohydrate overload" — he got into the grain bin, in other words. Just because he foundered doesn't mean he won't need his usual nutrients. And we don't want to starve him, for the reasons already given. He just needs the right nutrients delivered in a more balanced and natural way. He'll do just fine.

Vitamins

Here my advice is going to stir controversy. I advise you not to use vitamin mixes, free-choice or otherwise. These are concentrates and do not occur naturally in the wild. Very few foundered horses entering my care haven't been fed vitamin concentrates. So, I would be a little surprised if they didn't have a detrimental impact on the horse's digestive system. But why ponder or fret, when the natural alternative is so obvious and safe? Simply feed him natural fruits and vegetables!

Being vegetarians, horses love a range of delicious, vitamin rich plants. Wild horse country has a great variety (albeit scattered widely) of delectable and nutritious fruits, nuts, flowers, stems, bark, and so forth. Just look at the healthy family band of wild and "founder free" horses on the facing page. I've run my hand over the sleek beautiful coats and muscular bodies of wild ones like these. And they get that way from simple, basic, natural diets (and lots of natural movement). And nothing more.

Going "natural" is also inexpensive. Your foundered horse will think he's died and gone to heaven when you make haste from the supermarket or your garden with a range of fruits and vegetables. Following the same advice in feeding grains, dole out the fruits and vegetables in "nibble-size" portions, staggered throughout the day. Horses love carrots, apples, watermelon, and so on. Experiment. Bring home some broccoli, lettuces, squash, whatever. Chop it up so he can sink his incisors and molars into them. Give him only a handful or less at a time. Let him tell you what he likes. He's not stupid and will "kick out" what he doesn't want or need with his prehensile lips.

Incidentally, horses that eat "poisonous" plants will do this only when deprived of vegetation they prefer and need. Throw in a sugar cube or two now and then. Horses can have a "sweet tooth" just like people, and sugar is just as natural as the next plant. The famed Lippizaner stallions of the Spanish Riding School are fed sugary treats during training, and have been rewarded so for hundreds of years. And most of those high performance stallions are well into their twenties, and some into their thirties.

It won't take much to deliver his vitamin needs. You're not trying to "bulk" feed him, that's the job for the hay. So don't feed

Wild and founder free

SRP files

him a head of lettuce all at once, or a bag of carrots, or an entire watermelon. You'll just go broke overfeeding him. Horses are natural nibblers. Their tiny tummies were designed by nature for that purpose. So serve "mini" portions and do him and yourself a favor.

Minerals

I've already mentioned how the wild ones eat rocks to get at minerals they need. So, when I ask horse owners to leave rocks in their paddocks and fields, I really mean it in more than one way. The rocks not only provide abrasion to the hooves, and an obstacle course to encourage more natural motion, they may just be delivering vital nutrition as well. Grinding those rocks with their teeth is also nature's way of honing the teeth to rid them of bothersome sharp edges, thus making mastication more efficient and rendering food more digestible. I think of these sessions as wilderness "dental clinics."

On a related note, I also recall watching a monarch stallion nibbling on a clump of bunch grass one day. Part of the clump was near the nub, and having spent what seemed like an inordinate amount of time at the nub, my curiosity was finally aroused. Closer inspection revealed the stallion's tongue licking the earth around the base of the plant. More mineral nutrients, more dental work, more natural motion.

Realizing that many domestic horses probably don't have access — yet — to rocks and earth that can provide them with their mineral needs (and dental work), I've gravitated to those 50 lb. mineral blocks and salt licks (white or yellow). Throw them out there in the field or paddock and let the horse go at them. They'll lick and chew on them to get at those minerals/salt, and it's probably best for their teeth. Like hay, these are a 24 hr/day "free choice" part of the horse's natural diet.

Water

I've already discussed the value of water in conditioning the hooves. Of course, few horse owners would deprive their horses of free-choice water to drink, but what about foundered horses? Some horses are said to founder as a result of drinking too cold of water, or too warm, or water that isn't clear, or from drinking too much water, or drinking water after doing hard work, or from standing in cold water. Let's look at some of these claims.

In the wild, horses drink water at whatever temperature they find it at. This I've observed first hand. And it doesn't bother them. In fact, when water is scarce they will eat snow if it's available rather than leave a particular area of their range just for the sake of finding water to drink. This behavior is something I show horse owners in my seminars' wild horse movies.

In summer, wild horses will drink literally from muddy puddles. And that doesn't seem to bother them either. I once put my finger in such a puddle while a family band was watering, and that water was really warm. And it wasn't clear either. And there's no telling how many horses had been standing in it that day before we arrived.

Wild horses also survive on water pumped out of the ground into troughs by cattle ranchers leasing BLM land. Like the cattle, horses will go to these artificial sources if they're available. So I don't see any issue with drinking water from a trough, at least part of the time, in case some of you are wondering.

I'm not sure what it means when people suggest that horses can drink too much. How can anything exercising common sense, human, equine, or otherwise, drink too much water? Instinctively, horses know how much water they need, and that's how much they'll drink — if it's available. I've never known or heard of a wild horse drinking itself to death. I wouldn't do it, and I don't think the average horse is inclined to either.

Now what about drinking too much water, or too cold (or hot) of water, after a horse does hard work? I think the advice of marathon runners provides the perfect answer: don't deprive yourself of water when you're working your body hard. Which is to say, drink water as it is needed. Don't wait until your body is dehydrated to quench your thirst. When I was in the army years ago, they used to tell us, "It's better to drink the water in your canteen, than to die of thirst trying to save it." In the wild, horses instinctively "plan" their trips to watering holes to avoid dehydration.

How often they go depends on the temperature of the air, how much work they've done, or how long since they've been to the watering hole (also important is how eager they are to meet up with rival bands for "entertainment"). In other words, how thirsty they are. I've not known them to gallop five miles to get to a water hole. They "migrate" to and from them in an orderly manner. So maybe there's a warning there, of what not to do. The old saying, "cool your horse down and then let him drink," is probably sage advice if the occasion merits it. Indeed, common sense would suggest that dramatic temperature changes could throw a living thing's system into shock. But as far as foundering goes, I think it will take more than simple water to trigger a laminitic attack.

9 De-tox

I consider drug toxicity to be a subcategory of chemical pollution. Explore alternative treatments that reduce or eliminate the possibility of drug toxicity, which is the most common sin of commission of conventional medicine today. — Andrew Weil, M.D. (*Spontaneous Healing*)

I'm not really a "purist" like some holistic practitioners I know or have heard about, veterinary or medical. That is, I'm not entirely against using medicinal chemicals to heal with, and maybe use for preventive purposes. It just depends. But a foundered horse's healing may be hindered by chemical pollution, including prescription medications. So de-toxing your horse — flushing chemical toxins from his body — and maybe never using them again on him, could be an issue here. My rule of thumb is, if the horse doesn't need it, don't give it to him. Certainly the path to a chemical free life is enhanced by more natural and healthy living, and that's what this chapter is about.

Parasiticides

Since most horse owners seem to be using paste and feed-ration formulated wormers like crazy these days, this is an area of potential chemical overload. What effect they have on the horse's digestive system is something independent researchers ought to be looking at. Conceivably, the proliferation of harmful bacteria causing harmful enzymatic production at the laminar attachments could be stimulated or aided by these chemicals. Maybe the chemicals are killing off the "good" bacteria too, thereby destroying the balance and leaving the system open to toxicity — like a run down immune system.

It seems that most horse owners are swayed into using antiparasitic chemicals by fellow horse owners, their vets and the claims made on the wormer boxes themselves. Many can recount horror stories they've heard or read about of run-down "wormy" horses dying of colic precipitated by parasites. Some can even cite purported studies done by some university or another on the value and necessity of wormers. So, it's no wonder that many horse owners, dreading this microscopic invasion of their horse's well-being, just pull out all the stops and feed these strong chemicals as part of the horse's daily ration, whether they need it or not.

I believe this practice constitutes another founder trap. It's license to add yet another unnatural substance to the horse's already overloaded diet. Again and again, foundered horses brought to my attention are loaded with these chemicals, and I can't help but think they're part of the problem. Maybe a big part of the problem.

Paste wormer boxes are calculated to get into horse owner pocketbooks. No doubt to the tune of hundreds of millions of dollars every year, billions worldwide. There's a lot of economic incentive, it goes without saying, to convince horse owners that their equines need these products. To put all those harsh chemicals into their bodies.

I begin to have my doubts about parasiticides not long after I entered wild horse country. The occurrence of dung eating (coprophagous behavior), the ubiquity of stud piles visited by all the bands daily, and the presence of flies, coupled with healthy horses does make you wonder. Doesn't it?

In 1983, at one of the BLM wild horse processing stations, I got my first look at wild horse legs up close. Later, as I began to mingle with horses in their home ranges, I took further notice: the presence of bot eggs on their legs was as common as the setting sun. Why, they'd chew on them like they were candy! This led me to two startling conclusions:

> Parasites are perfectly natural to horses. Natural lifestyles keep parasites in balance.

So, to my way of thinking, it's not the presence of parasites that appear to harm domestic horses, or even that the parasites themselves kill our horses. Rather, it's the unnatural conditions horses must survive in that kill them. In opportunistic fashion, the parasites simply take advantage of the situation. They're there to end the horse's suffering.

So, what do we do?

Naturalize the horse's lifestyle. This book has been all about that so far. Try the things I've recommended – diet, healthy pastures/ paddocks, equine companions – all based on simulating healthy wild horse lifeways. Then start rolling back the chemical wormers.

Now, if your horse is definitely symptomatic of being wormy, and he's sick, then you'll need to worm him to clean the slate before beginning anew holistically. Chances are very good his diet is screwed up, or that he's too closely confined (i.e., a stall), that he's got no pasture time with other horses, not enough exercise, etc. These concerns aren't unimportant facets of the horse's life, they are what make a horse a horse. Deny them, and the parasites will rear their ugly little heads (not unlike the harmful bacteria waiting to sprout in the horse's digestive tract). Decide to battle with them on their level, with chemicals, and you're into the founder trap.

There are also natural "pesticides" (e.g., garlic) your horse can eat to help him balance out these pests. Follow the various educational materials in the Resource section, and they will lead you to them. But these are ancillary aids, not solutions. The solution is to reduce, and eliminate if possible, the level of unnatural chemicals in your horse's body. Naturalizing his lifestyle is the least expensive, safest way to accomplish this. And your horse will absolutely love you for letting him be himself.

Vaccinations

I'm afraid vaccinations may represent yet another founder trap. It's true that state laws compel us to protect our horses from harmful and communicable diseases, and vaccinations are an instrument of this effort. It is true too that we humans take vaccinations to prevent horrible diseases. Naturally, this practice is easily transferred to our horses.

Well, for one, horses are not people. Maybe they don't need them. And maybe we wouldn't either if humans lived more naturally, practiced better hygiene, and ate healthier foods. I'm thinking of the many native populations that existed here in North American before the encroachment of Europeans, and how many of them perished from diseases brought by Europeans. Accepting the inevitability of what happened, and speaking hypothetically, was the solution to vaccinate all the Indian people in advance of the invasion, or for Europeans to have "cleaned up their acts" before coming? It is a well known fact that many Europeans departing the Old World lived in unhealthy, overcrowded conditions, were the victims of poverty and political tyranny, were often sick with infectious diseases, seldom or never bathed, and knew nothing of balanced diets derived from good, wholesome food (including potatoes, corn, squash, tomatoes, beans, and many other foods which were introduced to them by native peoples).

It seems to me too that using chemicals to combat diseases that can be prevented by simply importing more wholesome lifestyle changes, is something worth considering.

I raise the "wild horse model" again, to demonstrate why it may not be necessary to inoculate every horse in sight. What is it about their lifeways that renders unnecessary routine vaccinations? Because if we cannot accept the possibility that there is a natural way that can work for our horses, then we've set one more founder trap to fall into. Again, more research in wild horse country seems reasonable in this regard.

In sifting through my founder consultations, I see that laminitic outbreaks do follow vaccinations. So this is something to think about. Don't you agree? I know the laws are there on the books concerning vaccinations, and that they govern our actions. But who wrote the laws, and who lobbied them into existence? What was their philosophy and what were their qualifications to assess more natural and healthier alternatives for our horses? Something to think about as we ponder the fate of our foundered horses at hand.

Antibiotics

Don't use them to treat laminitis unless your vet can confirm massive infection and your horse's life is imperiled for it. Don't use them preventively either.

Blood modifiers

The horse's blood is not the problem — so avoid all chemical therapies which aim to alter the horse's blood or circulation.

Thyroid medications

I've discovered a disturbing recurring relationship between foundered horses and thyroid medications. Thyroid imbalance will normally respond to naturalization of the horse's diet. My recommendation is to terminate their use immediately.

Chemical founder guards

Research is being conducted on new founder prevention medications. I don't believe in these because I don't believe they are necessary. The idea that people would douse their horses with preventative chemicals, rather than make very simple and inexpensive lifeway changes that preclude founder, seems short sighted and exploitative. How will Nature respond at deeper levels of science than we yet understand, if we subject a living thing to harmful management practices with stopgap chemical fixes that ignore causality. Let it be known here that in a private discussion I had with one of the world's leading laminitis researchers, he confided that he too shared grave concerns about this possibility.

Smart hooves

As we move further into this new millennium, the advent of genetic engineering will probably surface in one form or another in the fight against hoof problems. Thinking about this makes me wonder if "smart tissue" technology — the cloning of new organs, tendons, bones, etc. — won't have its impact on conventional founder therapy one day. I have no doubt that it will be applied to humans in replacing or repairing cancerous tissue, diseased blood, joint disorders, Alzheimer's Disease, and other "incurable" maladies, and, therefore, I have no reason to doubt that it won't transfer to horses with "bad hooves" in due time either. On the other hand, the saying "nature will find a way," is something I take as a stern warning, meaning causality is not inseparable from the laws of nature.

Holistic medications and therapies

My recommendation is to avoid them all (systemic medications), including the ersatz pain killers, in treating laminitis the natural way. Don't use acupuncture to treat laminitis or any other problem associated with the hoof. Don't use magnets on the hooves to treat laminitis.[†] Don't use body massage or chiropractic manipulations to treat laminitis or any problem associated with the hooves. Do not give oral drenches of any type to treat laminitis. Avoid all herbal feed additives that are non indigenous to wild horse country and proven to be safe.

Avoid any holistic "therapy" based on humans instead of horses. I take this position because: 1) I have no evidence that these alternative therapies work on horses; 2) I am concerned that they may pose a very real danger in interfering with the natural healing systems of the horse (e.g., powerful herbal pain killers that mask inflammation without the cause being removed); 3) They distract us from the real business at hand — restoring the natural lifeway of the horse and restoring the hoof mechanism (Here I am prepared to recommend one water-based balm to help moisturize the hooves with following removal of the periople during natural trimming); 4) Many of the people who have contacted me have dabbled in alternative therapies, all frustrated by their lack of success.

[†]As I discussed earlier in the book, veterinary efforts to increase circulation to the laminar attachments (stratum lamellatum) through vasodilation are not indicated in laminitis, since MMP proliferation is the issue and not availability of blood to the lamellatum basal cells. Some have argued, speciously in my opinion, that magnets can help increase blood circulation to the hooves, and, hence, promote healing in laminitis. Recognizing that we don't want to increase circulation within the hoof (which is the providence of the hoof mechanism), the question is moot. According to a study (Ramey, et al.) on the effects of magnetic leg wraps on circulation just released in the Journal of the American Veterinary Medical Association (2000; 217: 874-877), "application of the wrap for 48 hours had no effect on blood flow."

A true story

I'm calling to say that my horse has been pain free since July, and he can go barefoot on any terrain. — Lena to Jaime Jackson, December, 2000.

Bringing a severely foundered horse from the brink of death and onto the natural healing pathway can be a harrowing experience by all accounts. In the previous chapters, I discussed what I do holistically to stop the laminitic attack and prevent it from occurring. And it works. Holistically speaking, curing founder is a comprehensive process, a multi-faceted path culminating in a natural lifeway for the horse. Getting on the path is often an emotional and nerve wracking experience for horse owners deeply attached to their suffering equine companions. Especially when the horse's life is at stake. Since I frequently cope with this process myself as a holistic hoof care practitioner, I would like to share a "real life" experience with you in this final chapter. Maybe it will help you and your foundered horse find the strength to get on our natural healing pathway, regretfully still here at the fringe of conventional veterinary and farriery care as of this writing.

The following narration was written by myself, the horse's owner, Lena, and Marjorie, an amateur hoof care provider I sent to help Lena. Marjorie, like Lena, is a long time horse owner, who decided she wanted to become a natural hoof care provider. She studied our holistic hoof care movement's learning materials and attended one of my training clinics. Being an intelligent and thoughtful person, and caring of all horses, she put her mind and body to learning the trade. Marjorie happens to live in the northeast of the U.S., where she's been applying her newly acquired skills. When a founder case comes up in her area, it is my practice to call Marjorie in that she may conduct the trimming and give the horse owner emotional support as well.

Such was the case when Lena, a horse owner living in a state away from Marjorie called my office the day before her foundered horse, Joey, was scheduled to be euthanized at the recommendation of her vet. Joey, in excruciating pain, and virtually unable to stand, had been under the care of three vets and as many shoers before he broke down under a range of conventional treatments. In a last ditch effort to save the horse's life, Lena's son, Sven, turned to the Internet to find help for his mother's horse.

As he surfed the search engines, Sven delved deeper into the fringe, beyond the conventional therapies advertised on the farriery and veterinary websites. He knew these treatments not only didn't work, they had brought Joey to his deathbed. At the fringe, Sven eventually discovered the interconnections that led to me. It was simply a matter then of making a phone call, which Lena took upon herself.

Here's the rest of the story, garnered from our notes and diaries, in all our own voices, still unfolding as I type these words . . .

Lena

The stiffness seemed to settle in overnight. Joey, my 17 year old standard bred gelding walked on his box stall on October 1, 1999 with stiff, straight front legs. I immediately knew it was something very serious. My vet confirmed Founder in both front hooves after taking X-rays. The rotation of the coffin bone was minimal, but Joey was in a lot of pain. All grain was removed from his diet, and he was put on Bute (1 gram morning and night). He was also put on Tsoxsuprine tablets 30 (20 mg) AM and PM to increase the circulation to his hooves. I was told to keep Joey on strict stall rest for 3 weeks to see how he progressed.

At the end of 3 weeks he was still extremely sore, standing in the laminitic stance all the time looking totally depressed. He was rapidly loosing weight. I had to elevate his hay in a hay net since he was unable to eat his hay from the ground. I decided to let him out in the paddock with our two mares. It seemed to cheer him up a little, but the look of constant pain was clearly visible in his eyes, and it was breaking my heart. I sent Joey to a friend of mine for acupuncture treatments. There was no improvement. Joey was getting worse. In November I sought out a new vet who recommended corrective shoeing. Bar shoes were put on for a week but it just made him more uncomfortable. I had the bar shoes removed, and Joey was re X-rayed. The verdict was grim. Joey had a 14 degree and 15 degree rotation of the coffin bone in both front hooves. He stopped eating his hay. He was lying down most of the time. I started giving him 2 mg of Bute AM and PM in addition to the Tsoxsuprine. The vet advised me to put Joey down. I cried for two days. Then I made arrangements for the vet to come the following day. The grave was dug. The morning arrived, and Joey walked stiff legged out of the barn by himself as if to say "I am not ready to die yet". My son, Sven, called and advised "Don't put Joey down yet, let me look on the Internet". Thus began Joey's healing.

Sven found two opposing methods of curing laminitis. One recommended strict stall rest and corrective shoeing with an intricate wedge system and heavy wire to support the frog. Resection of the hoof wall was also recommended. The other alternate method to cure Founder used a systematic trimming of the hoof to restore it to its natural form without shoes. This system was based on restoring the hoof to resemble the hoof of the wild mustangs. I called Jaime Jackson, hoof care specialist, from Arkansas for a telephone consultation. This was October 24, the day before my birthday; and I was trying to save my horse's life. Joey had been my horse for 15 years. We had evented, fox hunted and done dressage together. The memories were overwhelming.

Jaime Jackson calmly reassured me that he thought Joey could be saved, but he told me that it would take a great commitment from Joey and me and that it would take 6 months to one year for Joey to heal. A whole new hoof would have to grow out.

A whole new living schedule was mapped out for Joey. Jaime

When I arrived, Joey was in founder stance (front feet way out in front of him) and had a kind but worried look in his eyes. The muscles in his rear end were quivering from the effort of leaning back. — Marjorie wanted Joey free to walk about at all times. No enforced stall rest. Joey was allowed to lie down when he wanted to, but he was to have total freedom to move if he so chose. A salt and mineral lick was to be available to him at all times. I was to offer Joey various vegetables, and he would pick out what he wanted. I was to feed him various kinds of grass hay-no alfalfa or clover. Jaime also recommended to take Joey off Bute and Tsoxsuprine as soon as possible to allow his body to heal naturally. Gradual trimming according to Jaime's wild horse hoof method was to be started.

Marjorie Smith, a hoof care specialist from Rhode Island was contacted and the first trim took place on December 7.

Marjorie

I met Joey the day he was supposed to be put down. The vet had done everything he knew how to do and it wasn't working.

His owner, Lena, felt strongly that Joey didn't want to die. So her son got on the Internet in a last-ditch effort to find help. Through Gretchen Fathauer's site on laminitis they got in touch with Jaime Jackson; Jaime called me that same night, and I went out in the morning.

Joey had been in a state of chronic founder for several months, and in addition the farrier had not been able to come, so his feet were about two months overdue. The farrier finally pulled the front shoes a few days before I came and trimmed the hoof walls right down to the sole.

When I arrived, Joey was in founder stance (front feet way out in front of him) and had a kind but worried look in his eyes. The muscles in his rear end were quivering from the effort of leaning back.

The first thing I did was pull the hind shoes. It took a while because Joey couldn't put the extra weight on his front feet for more than a few seconds.

Joey's front feet looked scary-awful. I'd been trimming my two horses' healthy feet for over a year under Jaime's guidance. This was only the second foundered horse I'd ever seen. His feet looked like blocks, very long and squarish, and totally flat on the sole because both coffin bones were rotated. There was almost nothing I could do without putting even more weight on the soles.

Joey could hardly pick up his front feet at all, he would begin to collapse from the pain. So I just nipped the tiniest bit off the heels. I had to go home with the "first trim" unfinished ~ I couldn't even rasp off the bumps from the nipper.

Lena

The first hoof trim was very painful for Joey. I had made the mistake of taking Joey off Bute too soon with the result that he was unable to lift any hoof off the ground for more than 5 - 10 seconds. Marjorie had to rotate around all feet continuously which made the trim a tedious process as well as a great deal of physical labor for Marjorie. With extraordinary patience and care a small amount of corrective trimming was done.

I was told Joey would be very sore for a few days after the trim. His heels were contracted (and he had grown an unusually long toe). It was going to take months for his hooves to become healthy and natural. But I had faith in Jaime and Marjorie. Every step was agony for Joey. I put him back on Bute, but left him off the Tsoxsuprine. Every week I cut down the Bute by 1/4 tab AM and PM. My guide was Joey. If he went off his hay, I knew I was going too fast. The key was to keep him comfortable enough to keep his will to live and to keep him walking. 1 had bought 16 rubber stall mats leading from the barn to the paddock. This made it easier for Joey to walk. Jaime instructed me to walk Joey for 5 to 10 minutes every hour.

Marjorie

For a week Lena walked Joey for 10 minutes every hour, all day long, to get the circulation going in his feet. When I came back he was still in founder stance, but was able to hold his feet up long enough for me to finish the "first trim" on all four feet. I kept telling Lena, "This isn't anywhere near what I'd like to get done, but the way this foot is, it's all I can do today." She would look, and agree, and we'd go on to the next foot. It was very humbling to have to make such small changes, when I wanted to help him so much.

Lena

After two weeks of walking him 5 minutes per hour from 6 AM to 7 PM at night, I was getting worn out mentally. Joey was lying down in between every 5 minute walk. I had to force him to move. This was the most difficult time for both of us. I increased his Bute to 1 1/2 gm AM and PM for 1 week. He was eating his hay again from a hay net or lying down. I had to bring him his hay and water where he stood or lay. He would not move on his own. I made a bed for him on the rubber mats in the barn, as well as outside, keeping just enough sawdust on the mats to absorb his urine. No deep bedding was allowed. It would create too much shearing of the sensitive lamina in his hooves.

Joey was kept loose in my 40 x 30 foot barn, able to walk up and down the aisle on rubber mats at will. I found that he liked to sleep on the rubber mat near the entrance to the barn with his head propped up in the sawdust pile. I had the hay and the water in 2 places near the sawdust pile and at the other end of the barn near his favorite mare "Mamma".

From his droppings I could see where he had traveled during the night. The first couple of weeks he remained in one area, near his favorite mare-then gradually he began to move more at night and he could eat off the ground in both hay areas, I was able to reduce the Bute to 1/2 gm AM and PM. Joey was now being walked 20 minutes 3 times a day on rubber mats, back and forth. Turning was difficult. It had to be very gradual and slow. I made sure to turn him left and right so as not to overstress any of the front hooves.

It was getting close to Christmas. The weather was cold and many times wet and snowy. The mats had to be shoveled and kept clean of debris. Any unevenness was agony for Joey. His hooves were soaked in 1/2 cup of apple cider vinegar and tepid water for 20 minutes per day. I looked at his hooves every day until I was dreaming about them. Jaime was my life line. "Don't even think about his feet" he would say. "Celebrate Christmas and Joey's Life". I did. Joey was slowly getting better. I gave him 2 small handfuls of whole oats, an apple and carrot in the AM and PM with Jaime's approval. The life spark was slowly coming back into Joey's eyes. The second trim took place on December 22. He was still very sore, He was still on 3/4 gm Bute Am and PM. If I lowered the dose, he stopped eating his hay.

Marjorie

When I came for the second trim three weeks later, Joey was no longer in founder stance. Lena had been walking him many times every day. He was able to hold his feet up a little longer for me to work on. I took a lot off the hind feet, which were still way over-long, hoping to make him more comfortable by bringing the base of the foot back underneath the legs.

A new horse arrived during Joey's second trim. When we put him back out in the paddock, he planted both front feet on the ground, swung himself around 180, and kicked both hind feet at the new horse. We whooped and cheered! Joey's life-attitude was terrific ~ this only a month after he would have been put down.

Lena

A big change happened on January 11, 2000 (3rd trim). He tolerated this well and ate hay the whole time. He is standing with his feet well underneath himself. No more laminitis stance. Soles on both front hooves are still dropped and both have slight indentations at the site of the coffin bones. Joey is still only able to walk on rubber mats, but his walk is normal

Marjorie

At the third trim, the front part of the sole on both front feet flaked off, leaving some vulnerable-looking, very stretched white line in the whole toe area. On one foot the coffin bone was right there in the bottom of a little groove; if I touched the groove with the hoof pick, he flinched.

There still was not much I could do with the front feet, though you could see the new hoof wall growing down from the hairline at a much better angle than the long, foundered toes. Again I was able to shorten the hind feet to make his back more comfortable. By this time, Lena was walking Joey for 20 minutes, three times a day, and he was walking around some on his own

Lena

Fourth trim on February 1. He tolerated the trim well, walking well on rubber mats. Soles are still sensitive. Some bleeding during the trim. Marjorie questioned if it was an old abscess. Soaking his feet daily.

Marjorie

On the fourth trim, we had a big surprise. There was some concavity appearing in the soles on the front feet! We fell into each other's arms and cried. It meant that the coffin bones were pulling up into a better position inside the hoof capsule, a big step in the healing process

Lena

Fifth trim on February 13. Great improvement noted. We noticed some concaving around the frog area in both front hooves. No bleeding. The new hoof angle is clearly visible. What a difference in Joey's attitude. He is now walking out of the barn by himself and into the field with the other horses. The new hoof was grown out almost 1 1/2 inches. On March 5 he was racing up and down the paddock, bucking and galloping. what a radical change.

Marjorie

On the fifth trim, the news was that Joey had gotten out and

At the third trim, the front part of the sole on both front feet flaked off, leaving some vulnerable-looking, very stretched white line in the whole toe area. — Marjorie *galloped* across the road to the neighbor's. He was also volunteering a trot and even a bit of canter in the soft, sandy arena. The new hoof walls by now were grown an inch down from the hairline; you could "see" the shape of the new, healed feet surrounded by the still scary-looking long toes. There was more concavity in the soles, and the grooves at the coffin bones were no longer painful.

I rocked him back more onto his heels and began to take off some of the extra toe length so the whole front wouldn't sheer off and leave him unprotected. Lena trimmed his hind feet herself, having practiced on another horse in the meantime.

Lena

Marjorie did the sixth trim on March 7. She was able to do a fair amount of trimming with the consequence that Joey was quite sore again for 10 days. However, he walked well on the mats, but no trotting at this time. The difficult part is for me to accept that after each trim there is a setback-but only to improve once more.

On March 22 I walked Joey on the lunge, he drew his head, bucked and took off trotting and cantering. I cautiously brought him back to a walk, not wanting him to overextend himself. According to Jaime, Joey will let me know what he is capable of doing.

Marjorie comes again on March 29. She wants to keep the trimmings three weeks 'apart, to allow for healing and growth. I helped trim Joey's back hooves last time. Marjorie is a wonderful teacher.

Joey has several more months to complete his healing, but he is "The Little Horse That Could". I am forever grateful to Jaime Jackson and Marjorie Smith.

Marjorie

This is where we stand at this writing. Joey is alive, and well on the way to being rideable again. I've learned a lot about the changes that occur in the hoof as it heals. I came to realize how serious laminitis is; Joey was living right on the edge for the first six weeks.

Joey 4th Feb

Rising dome effect

Joey 4th

On the fourth trim, we had a big surprise. There was some concavity appearing in the soles on the front feet! It meant that
the coffin bones were pulling up into a better position inside the
hoof capsule, a big step in the healing process. - Marjorie

Without Jaime's experience, confidence, and dietary knowledge, and Lena's devoted walking program, he probably wouldn't have made it, no matter how I trimmed his feet. I am awed and grateful to be part of Joey's recovery.

Jaime

Days before this book was to go to press (January, 2001), my office received a call from Lena. "Please tell Mr. Jackson that Joey has been pain free since July, and he can go barefoot on any terrain." She confided also that Lena and Marjorie have decided to write a book together about the experience of Joey's healing. Their hope — and mine — is that by going public they will be able to inspire others to do what they did. To seek a cure for founder in the natural healing lifeway of the horse.

The success of Joey's healing will remain contingent on Lena's faithful adherence to the principles of natural healing espoused in this book. Like a recovering alcoholic confronted with the possibility of "just one drink," there is no turning back. Ever. Eventually, the nightmare and memory of the founder horror will begin to fade into the past, where it belongs. The horse's natural lifeway is the key to keeping it there for good. In the name of humane care, each and every one of us owe it to our horses to put them on the same natural path as Joey's, for their own protection, and for our own piece of mind.

Founder Action Plan

If there is but one message or vital piece of information that can be borrowed from this little book, I hope it is an awareness that the cure and prevention of founder rests in simplifying the horse's lifeway. The horse is a simple animal with simple needs. To be healthy and founder-free, he needs only the basics: grass hay, water, and pasture time with other horses. He doesn't need shoes, a body full of chemicals, rich grains, rich hays, nor close confinement. Keep those things up — founder traps, in other words — and your horse will remain a walking time bomb.

Thank goodness, though, that the solution to the founder conundrum is a simple one. Because simplifying the horse's lifeway — making it more natural, to be exact — is a simple matter. It is the least inexpensive and the least traumatic of all conventional founder treatments. Your horse will love you for it!

Now, I recognize from lots of experience in helping horse owners professionally, that it may be a lot to ask you to commit all at once to naturalizing your horse's lifeway. Especially in the middle of a founder attack. So at least consider making changes gradually and with understanding.

Start first with lifestyle changes that are urgent and that will counter the most egregious and dangerous founder traps. Phase out these troublemakers quickly, and supplant them with healthy alternatives described in the previous chapters. These will bring you and your horse badly needed relief and pave the way for healing. Other changes can be planned for and dealt with as the founder attack is turned back, and the first twinges of soundness are apparent. Once healing has begun, you'll want to capitalize on the early successes by reinforcing them with other long term lifestyle changes that will insure permanent soundness and prevent founder from striking again.

Making gradual changes is also easier on the horse. Their bodies, and particularly their hooves, seem most vulnerable when we make radical changes in their lives, such as diet and hoof care. But sometimes we do harm by slowly building up toxins in their systems or by gradually deforming the shape of their feet through unnatural trimming methods. So founder traps can be built in both ways: quickly and more slowly over the long term. But by understanding how to naturalize the horse's lifeway, the task of dismantling the founder traps is really straightforward. We can "bring" the horse back into a more natural lifestyle without causing further stress on his already taxed system.

I'm emphasizing gradual changes here because the path out of the founder traps will require *your* patience, understanding of the issues, and time. Allow your horse as much time to get out of the traps as it took to put him in them. Implement the holistic changes and then let them do their work for you. Don't rush matters, let them unfold at the speed nature accords them to effect actual healing. Natural healing occurs at its own speed. Believe in the incredibly powerful forces of your horse's natural healing system.

The promise of "quick fix" treatments through conventional and invasive (chemical, surgical, and orthopedic) veterinary and farriery care, or by charlatan "holistic equine practitioners" who've never trimmed a horse in their life, can be very seductive. But they are invariably palliative, and sometimes pathogenic in themselves, and will bring no lasting cure if the necessary natural lifestyle changes are not addressed. So avoid them. Conversely, avoid practitioners who won't promise anything except uncertainty, a 50/50 chance, and a billing statement.

Prognosis

Foundered horses can be rendered sound and rideable within days (very unusual), weeks (unusual), or months (common). The characteristic founder hoof (slipper toe, fescue foot, etc.) may take another 9 months or longer to "work out" of the capsule. Ride any foundered horse as soon as healing is substantiated, in other words, if he can walk, trot, canter, whatever, without coming up lame. I don't believe in coddling the hooves of any horse, including those that are foundered. If he's sound enough to walk normally, he's ready to ride.

Of course give extra leeway for horses with hoof slough, since a new hoof wall will have to grow in where there was none. In cases where the coffin bone has penetrated the sole, delay riding until the bone has re-ascended into the capsule and concavity of the solar dome has been reestablished. Look at the bottom of the hoof to ascertain this, you don't need x-rays. Speaking of which . . .

X-rays

This may come as a surprise to you the reader, but I don't believe in using x-rays with foundered horses because they aren't necessary. They're a waste of money and time. And they can mislead you into doing all sorts of terrible things to your horse, as I've discussed in this book already. What can they tell you except what common sense and your own two eyes should make perfectly clear? "Fear of coffin bone rotation" lies at the bottom of the current hysteria and obsession with x-rays. But I don't care how much rotation there is, all the x-rays in the world aren't going to stop it or make it better. The only thing that's going to make it better is to make the necessary natural and holistic changes in your horse's life this book calls for.

Go barefooted

This is a big one with me. It's time that horse owners like yourself start thinking about riding your horse unshod or with hoof boots. That's right, without horseshoes! What you probably don't realize, or maybe you do by now, is that your horse's feet can be conditioned to ride without any protection in most terrains. Start looking into this right away. Before you consider re-shoeing your horse, check out the Resources section of this little book. It'll get you started down the barefoot path. You'll discover that your horse will move better than ever once he's liberated from those horseshoes and his feet are given genuine natural trims and fitted with quality riding (not medicine) boots. And he'll love you for not having to put up with all that hammering on his feet.

Use hoof boots for riding

As more and more horse owners turn to barefootedness, we're all going to see more and more "hoof boots" come into the hoof care marketplace. This is already beginning to happen in the U.S., and it is a very exciting and important development.

Here I am speaking of a well-made riding hoof boot that properly fits the horse's foot, stays on, and can be put on or removed easily. It will enable you and your horse to ride anywhere, anytime, while your horse's feet are conditioning to go barefooted. Riding boots will also free you from expensive shoeing bills in the future, not to mention vet bills that entail harmful and unnecessary orthopedic shoeing.

As explained earlier, use hoof boots to help transition your foundered horse to soundness. Just as soon as possible, have him fitted correctly and then use the boots during rehabilitative exercises only, removing when he is at liberty. Never leave boots on a foundered horse 24 hours a day.

Become a natural rider

Learning to ride your horse "naturally" isn't a mythical or fantasy subject. It is the true "art of horsemanship" that so many horse owners have heard or read about, but never seen. It has nothing to do with dressage, or English, or Western, riding; yet, properly done, it has or can have much to do with all of them. I've included one book, the only book I'm aware of, in the Resource section to get you going as a natural rider. The authors, British ladies, have developed an extensive seminar network to give you hands-on-training here in the U.S.

Founder Checklist

Finally, to conclude this book, I've included a "Founder Healing Pathway Chart" (pages 150-151) — a summary of the holistic principles espoused in this book for preventing and curing founder the natural way. Take your founder horse through it and you will reap success and soundness.

For healthier and more natural founder-free horses,

Jaime Jackson

(overleaf) Founder Healing Chart

Founder Diagnosis

A founder diagnosis should be made by a licensed veterinary equine practitioner.

Founder

Diet

While your hoof care professional takes care of the hooves, work immediately on changing your horses diet.

Do's

- ☑ Provide multiple free choice grass hays
- ☑ Feed oats, whole or crimped
- ☑ Provide drinking water at ground level
- ☑ Give fresh fruits and vegetables
- ☑ Provide free choice mineral block
- ☑ Provide free choice salt block

Dont's

- ☒ No legume or fescue hays
- ☒ No green grass at any time
- ☒ No sweet feeds
- ☒ No vitamin concentrates

Boarding

Most founder cases will require immediate changes in their living quarters.

Do's

- ☑ If your horse is in pasture, remove him at once to a paddock with a connected covered stall
- ☑ If your horse is stalled, provide him with a paddock turnout connected to a covered stall
- ☑ Provide rubber mats, lined in rows for exercise
- ☑ Provide all dietary necessities within his boarding quarters
- ☑ Provide foot bath for hooves
- ☑ Keep him in constant contact with one or more horse buddies

Dont's

- ☒ No pasture turn out or access to green grass of any type from any source
- ☒ Do not confine to a stall

Healing Chart

De-tox

During the laminitic attack and during the healing phase, minimize the use of any drugs. Avoid all invasive surgical procedures.

Do's

- ☑ If necessary (i.e., horse refuses to eat or drink, makes no effort to move, low pain tolerance), use Phenylbutazone ("bute") prescribed by your vet to control pain:
  - Follow 3 days on/1 day off cycle

Dont's

- ☒ No antibiotics
- ☒ No chemical inhibitors
- ☒ No vaccinations
- ☒ No blood modifiers
- ☒ No parasiticides
- ☒ No vitamin shots
- ☒ No thyroid medications
- ☒ No homeopathic medications
- ☒ No tenotomies to relieve coffin bone tension
- ☒ No toe wall resections
- ☒ No coronary grooving
- ☒ No surgical drains
- ☒ No x-rays

Hooves

Provide natural hoof care at once.

Do's

- ☑ Remove horseshoes
- ☑ Give hooves natural trim
- ☑ Keep horse barefooted at all times except when booted
- ☑ Trim at 3 to 4 week intervals
- ☑ Fit hooves with riding boots as soon as horse can stand to be fitted. Use boots only when:
  - horse is still too sore to walk barefooted
  - riding after healing phase
- ☑ Soak hooves daily in water or clean mud for 10 minutes
- ☑ Soak hooves in mild vinegar solution if WLD is diagnosed (see page 86-87 for instructions)
- ☑ Use water based hoof penetrant once after each trim (see Resources)

Dont's

- ☒ No standard (keg) or orthopedic shoes (e.g., bar shoes)
- ☒ No glue-on shoes
- ☒ No pads
- ☒ No foam sole support devices

Resources

The following list of learning materials and products are available from the Star Ridge Company. Call 1-870-743-4603 or visit their website at www.star-ridge.com

Natural Horse Care

The Natural Horse by Jaime Jackson. 1992 (1st. ed.), 1997 (2nd ed.)

Natural Hoof Care

Horse Owners Guide to Natural Hoof Care by Jaime Jackson. 1999.

"Creating the Perfect Hoof: Learn To Do A Natural Trim With Jaime Jackson". 2000. (Companion video to *Horse Owners Guide to Natural Hoof Care* by Jaime Jackson)

How to Boot horses

Guide To Booting Horses For Natural Hoof Care Practitioners book/companion video by Jaime Jackson. 2001.

Natural Hoof Care Clinics

Jaime Jackson Natural Hoof Care Clinics: www.jaime-jackson.com

American Association of Natural Hoof Care Practitioners (AANHCP): www.AANHCP.org

Star Ridge Natural Hoof Care Bulletins

It is a fact that adherents of natural horse care are always seeking new information to help improve their skills and the lives of their horses. In the ongoing effort to clarify the meaning of natural hoof care and to bring practitioners and horse owners to standard on the most current information available,

(Continued on page 152)

natural hoof care products

SERVING THE NATURAL HOOF CARE COMMUNITY SINCE 1997

www.star-ridge.com

(Continued from page 152)

Jaime Jackson and Star Ridge Publishing have put together the new **Natural Horse Care Resources** bulletin series.

Each bulletin is a highly detailed, comprehensive article about very specific facets of natural hoof care and horsekeeping practices that concern serious practitioners. These are "action" articles, intended to help readers think through the issues and to "act" on the information in practical ways. Many were inspired by questions raised repeatedly by horse owners and practitioners who felt that some issues needed more in depth treatment or clarification. Others arose simply because new information, research, and technical breakthroughs rendered them relevant.

The SRP bulletins are replete with vividly clear, colorful photographs and line drawings in a striking, professional format. New, stepwise trimming descriptions are presented in Jaime Jackson's familiar style that readers have come to know and trust. All the bulletins are closely related and are designed to work together in an integrative manner with Jaime's videos and books. "The *HOG*," notes Jaime, "was written to provide general or foundational guidelines for natural hoof care. The bulletins, in contrast, are designed and organized to take practitioners to deeper levels of understanding, nuance and practical application . . . to add clarity of purpose, to challenge potential misunderstandings and troublesome areas, and to incorporate new and significant information. They also represent my latest thinking — in more ways than one, we go to the very cutting edge of the natural hoof care movement, where all serious practitioners should be heading." Let the SRP **Natural Horse Care Resources** bulletin series challenge you to become a better practitioner or advocate of the natural path.

On the following pages are descriptions of Jaime's new "laminitis/ founder" articles in the SRP Bulletin series. These include Jaime's latest information on healing laminitic horses, and provide explicit instructions for trimming acute and chronic laminitic hooves according to the principles of natural hoof care. These bulletins are available only from Star Ridge. Call or visit the SRP website to place your order: **www.star-ridge.com**

New! Star Ridge "Laminitis" Bulletin Series

#102/*Supercoriaitis*: Laminitis Redefined. Jaime believes that current epidemic levels of "laminitis" seen around the world are compounded by our very definitions of what this word is alleged to mean. Arguing that the term "laminitis" is essentially incorrect, incomplete, and misleading, Jaime provides an alternative conceptualization for the age old hoof disease — and a new definition. "Until practitioners and horse owners accept the fact that laminitis is not what they think it is," states Jaime, "horses will continue to succumb and die from it in staggering, ever-increasing numbers." (10 pp.)

#103/The Supercoriatic (Laminitis) Pathway. Having redefined the term laminitis in B#102, Jaime turns to the disease itself and traces its causality and destructive path. Jaime: "I'm in complete disagreement with the diagnosis, treatment, and prognosis of laminitis offered up by our veterinary community. The pathogenesis of laminitis need not be an incomprehensible labyrinth leading to breakdown or euthanasia. The path is a "straight arrow" from prevention to cure." (8 pp.)

B103/Figure 2 This Supercoriatic hoof had been shod for two years and refused to heal before being brought into natural hoof care.

#104/Trimming the Supercoriatic (Laminitic) Hoof. The purpose of this article is to show how to adapt the natural trim to the laminitic hoof. States Jaime, "I used to think that everyone would readily see how simple it is to give a laminitic hoof a natural trim. Now I see that, with few exceptions, most practitioners — particularly untrained vets, farriers, and beginners in natural hoof care methods —

(Continued on page 157)

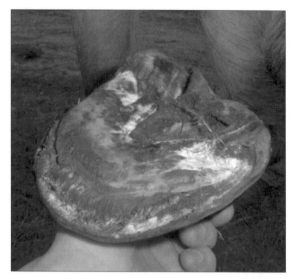

B#102/Figure 6 This Supercoriatic (laminitic) hoof is well on the road to recovery following a strict regimen of natural boarding and trimming, the latter conducted at 4 week intervals. (*Top*) Before first trim; after 10th trim. The pony, previously completely lame, had been earmarked for euthanasia; now trots and gallops soundly.

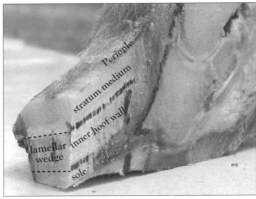

Cross-section of laminitic hoof showing lamellar wedge. [Bul. #104]

(Continued from page 155)
panic and quickly abandon the natural trim when confronted by the terrifying laminitic profile. With their skeletal methodology in compromise or outright chaos, hoof care is reduced to worrisome happenstance. Chronic laminitis, or worse, then ensues. Many then abandon the effort and fall back upon a predaceous conventional veterinary and farriery community, which chastises them for having 'gone natural' in the first place. Part of this failure stems from not understanding the Supercoriatic pathway [B#103] and how it can undermine even the most competent practitioner's efforts. But by far the biggest problem contributing to failure, in my opinion, is the practitioner's problematic attempts to render a natural trim without actually understanding the wild horse hoof model upon which natural hoof care is entirely based. Not surprisingly, *failure is inevitable*." (14 pp.)

Order all SRP Bulletins at www.Star-Ridge.com

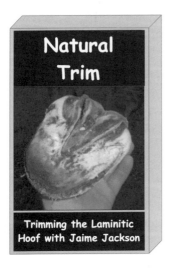

Natural Trim: Trimming the Laminitic Hoof with Jaime Jackson

Learn how to trim laminitic hooves with master trimmer Jaime Jackson. Jaime brings to bear his entire arsenal of information and technique to put laminitic hooves on the road to healing and soundness. Use with companion bulletin. VHS, NTSC, 1 hr.

order at www.Star-Ridge.com

Index